Happy to be Here

Selected Facebook Posts

by

ELIZABETH BERG

A *W*RITING *M*ATTERS PUBLICATION

ISBN: 9781078467599

Author's Website: www.elizabeth-berg.net

Book Design by Phyllis Florin

Happy to be Here

Phyllis and I are so happy to offer another Happy book! And this one, like the others, comes with this advice: It's best to read one a day. We hope you'll enjoy the reads!

Changes

I remember being a young girl, lying in the bathtub and seeing that my knees were not my knees. Or so it seemed. They had changed, somehow, when I wasn't looking, had become what I thought of as "horsier," whatever that meant. But then those were the days I thought breasts were called "hoo-hoos." My mother corrected me one night—coincidentally while I was in the bathtub—and she was kneeling beside me to help me wash up. "They are called *breasts*," she said. And I said, "...Really?" I wasn't quite sure she was right, but in the end decided I had to take it on her authority.

Yesterday, I went to a yoga class. I hadn't been to one in a long time, and I've always enjoyed the benefits of a good yoga class, provided I can at least attempt some of the poses. The instructor began with a guided meditation. Who doesn't like a good guided meditation? Well, me, apparently, because suddenly, I didn't like the meditation, and I didn't want to go along with it. My scofferator was turned up to high. I wouldn't let in her suggestions; I wouldn't even close my eyes. Instead, I looked around at all the other people with their eyes closed, a look of peace upon their faces, and I thought, Hmmm. Should I make eggplant parmesan for dinner or salmon?

About ten or fifteen minutes later, the first pose was demonstrated, and I did it for a while, but then I just quietly rolled up my mat, gathered up my belongings, and crept out of the room. I was enormously relieved. I felt like I'd just escaped from something.

Next, I marched into the business office of the gym and announced that I wanted to cancel my membership. The guy I spoke to had cottage cheese, blueberries and strawberries on his desk. I thought, See? See what a healthy snack he's having? This is a good place! It promotes healthy habits! But I quit. When the guy asked why I was canceling my membership, I said, "You know, I just don't get here. Every month, I pay my fee, but I never get here. I came the other day after a long absence and you know what I did? I got a massage! That was my 'exercise,' a massage!" We had a little laugh about that. Then the guy told me I could still come for a massage as a nonmember and that I could use the gym for free on those days. Now there's some incentive, I thought. But kind of expensive incentive.

When I got to my car, I sat there for a moment thinking, *How odd. How odd that I just did that.* When I walked in, I had no intention of quitting the class or the gym. Yet I felt I'd done the right thing.

When I was in my twenties, I all of a sudden up and left a job as an editorial secretary. I walked home, and I remember going across a bridge, looking up at the birds flying free, and feeling absolutely exhilarated. I had no prospects for another job. My then-boyfriend told me I was nuts to leave that job, it was a *good job*!! (Not really, but never mind.) But something in me told me to get up and go that day, and I got up and went, and I never ever, ever regretted it, not even when I was left with one dollar to my name. (I used that dollar to buy a rose that I left on a rock as an offering in my favorite little park.)

It may be that I've come to a time in my life where I'm being more discerning about what I put on my plate. I don't have room for everything I used to do, plus the new things I've added. It has come time to eliminate some things (things that don't "spark joy," it occurs to me to say), and it appears that since I didn't consciously acknowledge that, my subconscious cleared its throat and said *"Elizabeth? They are called* breasts," if you know what I mean. My subconscious presented a reality I've been dodging.

Sometimes I forget that people are always changing. Sometimes it's slowly, other times it's all of a sudden, and I guess I believe we do well to go with that flow, so long as it's not harmful to us. I want more time to read Katherine Mansfield, to reflect, to spend time with friends and my grandchildren. I want to be able to look out the window at the snowflakes flying around as though there's an enormous game of tag going on, to walk Gabby to the bookstore and leaf through a stack of possibilities before choosing one. Or two. Or three.

You know, when I left that yoga class, I was feeling a weird kind of anger. And I think I manufactured that anger so that I would have an excuse for wanting to leave. But anger didn't need to be the motivation. Awareness should have been the motivation. Acceptance. Willingness to change. Today, the day after the big quit, I'm there.

Motels

Today, December 12, the first motel opened in
1925. Now that is a day that should be honored.
As an Army brat, I spent a lot of time on the road.
I rode in the back seat, usually by a window, the
better to play Auto Bingo, and inhaled Camel
cigarette smoke from my father puffing and puffing and puffing away. In would go the cigarette
lighter, out would pop a glowing coil, and he'd
start another one. My Dad liked to "make time," as
he called it, so we often pulled into motels quite
late at night. For me, it was like dragging my
sleepy self into paradise. Look! A "Magic Fingers"
bed! Look! Little tiny bars of soap, and towels and
wash clothes you'd never seen before that were
all folded up and waiting for you. Look! A paper
band around the toilet seat, making it seem as if
no one had ever used it before, ever! And swimming pools, oh my. If the motel had a swimming
pool I'd figure it was equivalent to a movie star's
home. I'd settle into bed, and I would feel like I
was still moving. When I woke up in the morning,
there was the promise of breakfast out. I loved
breakfast out, and I still do. The yellow of the
yolks, the crispness of hash browns, the wait staff
filling coffee cups again and again, the jokey
banter unique to that time of day, the newspapers
spread out on tables.

There are restaurants who, in their infinite
wisdom, serve breakfast 24 hours a day. When I
grow up, I want to live between a motel and one
of those restaurants. And if the restaurant menu

has a rooster on the menu, standing on top of a hen house to crow while behind him the morning sun rises in a pink and yellow sky... well, my happiness will be complete.

Sewing Machine Blues

When I was eight or nine years old, I tried sewing for the first time. I made a pair of pink pedal pushers for my Ginny doll. Each stitch was roughly the length of the Mississippi River. Also, the stitches were on the outside. I didn't know how in the world you would get stitches to be on the inside. Stick your hand down there and sort of sew in the dark? The notion of turning the pants inside-out did not present itself as a solution to me. I was then and am now rather literal-minded. And I was horrible on those tests where you had to kind of deconstruct and/or reassemble. Remember those tests?

Ginny's pedal pushers were too tight in the leg and too big at the waist. They had to be big at the waist, since there was no closure: no button or zipper, not even scotch tape. (It occurs to me that we're so free-wheeling now in fashion, such wild and crazy guys, that I could make a pair of ill-fitting pink pedal pushers for myself with no closures and with the stitching on the outside; wear them with a certain amount of hostile confidence, like a model, or like those guys whose pants are always just about falling down; and they could become a Thing.)

I believe I may have attempted to make a blanket out of Kleenex next, and then I kind of gave up. I did long for one of those baby sewing machines, which I thought might magically make me a sewer, but I never got one, even as I never got an

Easy Bake Oven, which I will *never* stop complaining about.

I eventually bought myself a machine and tried to make a few things. At the time, I was singing in a band at night and also had a day job as a secretary in a fabric warehouse, and I got free fabric. I made up a yellow tunic top with bell bottom pants and actually wore it on stage. No buttons, no zippers, *that was* too hard. The top went over my head and there was a narrow band of fabric at the back to keep the thing together. God only knows what I used to keep the pants up. Probably ribbon.

Next I tried to reupholster my sofa. *That* went about as well as you might expect.

When I was living with the man who would become my husband, I made him the ugliest brown jumpsuit in the world. Uglier than what you're imagining right now and even more ridiculous. I had a pattern, but the directions only pissed me off because they were incomprehensible, as I saw it. I threw away the directions and cut out the pattern, minus those little triangles because what the heck were THEY there for? Then I tried to put the thing together, which I sort of succeeded in doing. My boyfriend, bless his heart, gamely tried it on, and then I threw it away.

When my first daughter was born, I became interested in trying to make clothes for her. I remember buying some tools for sewing and how the saleswoman said, staring right at my husband, that I *had* to have a *good* pair of scissors. She was absolutely right. And I did get a good pair of scissors. Also, I began figuring out what the patterns were talking about. I made a lot of cute things for my daughter: skirts, pants, nightgowns, quilts. I still make quilts, kind of awful ones, and I make stockings for people at Christmas.

I will never be a good sewer. That's okay. I just like it.

Last night, a man who was probably in his seventies came over to fix my sewing machine. He sat with my ailing 25-year-old Viking Husqvarna and talked about how they don't make those machines in Sweden anymore, how they aren't as good as they used to be, mine was a really fine machine. And indeed, I've never needed a repair until now. I watched his hands as he fiddled around with it, and I talked to him about how he came to do this line of work. He used to sell Vikings, he said, and now he makes house calls to fix all kinds of sewing machines. He was such a sweet man. Gabby kept coming up and laying her head in his lap and he didn't mind at all. Also, he was totally Zen when we uncovered what looked like the remnants of a mouse nest under something on my sewing table. It must have been from a time when we had a number of the little visitors. I was completely embarrassed and rushed to clean everything up, but he was fine, just told me about how mice can actually get in sewing machines and set up shop there.

I thought it was a miracle that you could get someone to come to your house to fix your machine, and I told him so.

He just smiled. He said, "If you ever need service again, just call me." He gave me his card. I said, "Okay, I'll call you again in 25 years." He just smiled at that, too.

I watched him disappear into the night, with his wonderful tools all kept in a rolled up piece of fabric.

Lots of times, things fade or disappear and you aren't quite aware of it until it's gone. Not this time. I don't think there will be anyone taking this guy's place. And we're all poorer for it, even if we don't sew.

Car Wash Fear

I have a lot of irrational fears. Bananas, because when I was a girl, someone told me that poisonous spiders live on them and they are the same *exact* color of the banana and you can *never* see them and they will *paralyze* your throat. I fear rushing sewer drains. I fear the cordials in the candy box—nope, not gonna eat them. I fear centipedes, as has been well documented on this Facebook page. I fear the tools the people who do pedicures use, especially when they are holding a really medieval looking thing that may or may not have been sterilized properly and they look up at you and say, "Short?"

But the biggest fear I have is of car washes. I fear:

— That the line will be super long and I will have forgotten to bring a book to read.

— The person who waves me forward to get my tire onto whatever that metal thing is so I'll be pulled into the car wash. I especially fear that person when they get impatient with me for going so slow because I fear my tire will NOT get on correctly and the tire will get all torn up and then the undercarriage; and then the whole car, wanting in on the party, will just dissemble itself around me. And all the people behind me will swear at me and honk at me to get out of the *way*.

— I fear my car is not in neutral even though I put it in neutral.

— I fear I don't really have my windshield wipers off even though I turned them off.

— I fear my windows are not rolled all the way up even though I rolled them all the way up.

— I fear I'll get stuck in there during the mighty suds cycle.

— I fear I'll engage the car and start driving out too soon even though I never drive out until the green light says, "Good Lord, girl, what do I have to do to tell you to put your car in *gear* and get *out*?"

— I fear that the people who dry off the car will use dirty towels, which, I'm sorry, they always do. Every time.

I could rewash the car, but......you know.

Cookies!

Another gray day. And a cold, cold rain. What does this mean? It means I make a new cookie recipe—Cranberry Nut Cookies. These are nice and tart *and* sweet. I hope I don't eat them all, as the reason I made them was to give them to my neighbor, who snow blows my sidewalks for me all the time. What a good guy.

Note to self: Stay in study. Do *not* go in kitchen. Even if there is a fire, do not go down to the main floor to escape because you will take all the cookies with you. Escape from your office window.

Cranberry Nut Cookies

Note: You can chop up the cranberries in your food processor, you don't have to cut them all in half one by one. Unless you want to zone out.

2/3 cup butter, softened
1 cup sugar
1 cup packed brown sugar
1 large egg
1/4 cup 2% milk
2 tablespoons lemon juice
3 cups all-purpose flour
1/4 cup ground walnuts
1 teaspoon baking powder
1/2 teaspoon salt
1/4 teaspoon baking soda
2-1/2 cups halved fresh or frozen cranberries
1 cup chopped walnuts

1. In a large bowl, cream butter and sugars until light and fluffy. Beat in the egg, milk and lemon juice. Combine the flour, ground walnuts, baking powder, salt and baking soda; gradually add to the creamed mixture and mix well. Stir in the cranberries and chopped walnuts.

2. Drop by heaping tablespoonfuls two inches apart onto lightly greased baking sheets. Bake at 350° for 16-18 minutes or until golden brown. Remove to wire racks to cool.

Makes five dozen.

Source: www.tasteofhome.com

Memories

Many of you know that I grew up an Army brat. Whenever we were living in the states, we used to go to Minnesota for summer vacation. We didn't stay together once we got to Minnesota; rather we kids were sent to various relatives' houses. When I was younger, I used to stay with my Aunt Lala and Uncle French, and their kids. We often arrived there very late at night, and I would be ushered up to a bed that had been made up with sheets that had dried on the line, and the smell was intoxicating: captured sun and wind.

My best memories of staying there are when the grown-ups would all be in the kitchen drinking coffee and talking (or the men watching the fights on the black and white TV and drinking Hamms beer while the women stayed in the kitchen, drinking coffee and talking). There would be a big box of donuts on the counter, left open, which only invited the inevitable, namely us kids eating as many donuts as we possibly could, and then some.

We kids would hang out on the big, screened-in front porch where we would loudly carry on and I used to laugh so hard my gut hurt. I particularly liked when we got in a big pile and punched each other. Also I liked the time one of my cousins carefully lined up shoes along the top of a bedroom door and then called hysterically, *"Dad! Dad!"* and the dad rushed upstairs and pushed open the door and all the shoes fell on his head. I have no explanation for why I loved this so much, when I am so anti-violence now.

I do still love peanut butter and pickle sandwiches, as I did then, though, and I think I'll go and make one now. Also, I still love the smell of lake water and the idea of Fourth of July picnics. Well, I love the idea of picnics at any time of year which begs the question: why is the beautiful picnic hamper I bought in the garage being enjoyed only by spiders?

Weight Watching

When I was attending Weight Watchers meetings, I used to like the true confessions part. My favorite was when someone said there was chocolate cake sitting on her counter when she got up in the morning and she threw it in the garbage. Everyone cheered. Then she said, all small-voiced, "But then I pulled it out and ate it." I cheered.

It is in that spirit that I share the following:

I am gaining weight like a sponge taking up water. And so the night before last, I vowed to *stop eating carbohydrates*. The next morning, I had avocado toast, because it's not really bread, it's avocado. For lunch, I had a "Parisian" sandwich, which was ham and cheese and lettuce on a baguette, and I asked for extra mayo. Then I asked Bill if he was going to eat the bread that came with his salad and he said no so I said, okay, I'll give it to Gabby, but I ate it. In the afternoon, I went to a movie by myself, *Dunkirk.* Bill didn't want to see it because it had gotten so many bad reviews online. Do not listen to those bad reviews. The movie is a masterpiece. It's like a fugue. It's absolutely beautiful and wrenching. All the way home on my bike I had to fight to keep from sobbing. It shows war in a kind of 360-degree way I've never seen before.

But the point in telling you this is that I ate popcorn in the movie. With a bunch of fake butter. Also I had a few Junior Mints because I was trying to be good and not eat bread.

For dinner, we went out for Italian because I had been reading Italian recipes and I had to go and eat Italian. I thought, well, I'll get Chicken Limone and salad and I did, but also I ate three (3) pieces of bread that I dragged through olive oil and Parmesan cheese. And the side of spaghetti that I asked for. When I got home I ate some of that dang buttermilk raspberry cake.

So. You know.

Today I got up and ate yogurt only and took Gabby for a fast 45-minute walk and I'm having salad for lunch and fish and vegetables for dinner and I'm putting that dang buttermilk raspberry cake in the freezer. Right after I have a piece.

Walking

It was George Sand who said that she took walks for the spirit as well as—if not more than—the body. Probably a lot of people say that, or, if they don't say it, feel it.

I'm just back from a longish walk with Gabby. We passed the chickens that live around the corner from me, uncharacteristically silent today. "Buk-buk-buk-*awk*?" I said, but got no response. Not a peep. So to speak (though these hens are far past the peep stage). Maybe they were watching a movie or meditating.

We passed the Swiss chard growing in someone's boulevard garden which I am always so tempted to pick a little of but never do. We passed the site of the most magnificent garden I have ever seen in my life that now lies in ruins, most of it dead, courtesy of the people who bought the house after the gardener extraordinaire moved away. Going past that garden is an exercise for me in trying to be nonjudgmental. So far it's not going so well, because so far every time I pass it a voice in my head screams, *Why did you people let the garden go like this?????* Plus anyone I'm walking with has to hear the story of how there used to be the most beautiful garden here. What business is it of mine how the people who live there want to maintain (or not) their garden? What do I know of their reasons? Live and let live, says a little voice in my brain which needs to get to be a bigger voice.

Gabby and I went through Scoville Park and there was the homeless guy I see a lot and call

Surfer Dude because he reminds me of one of those blond, sun-kissed guys who seem perpetually all right with the world. I'm dying to talk to him, but I'm too shy. But today he saw me and smiled and then I smiled back and said, "Do you like dogs?" He shrugged. "They're all right," he said, and then I couldn't think of anything to say back so I offered the all-purpose, "Oh, uh huh," and Gabby and I kept walking.

We passed stores and restaurants, and I read menus displayed in the windows as if I haven't read them a bazillion times already. We passed the Metra train and bells were ringing, *clang clang clang*, very exciting. We passed Scratch 'n Sniff, the dog and cat store and Gabby stood hopefully at the entrance but they weren't open yet. We went over to Austin Gardens Park and there, there, there he was. The magnificent Milo. A male Golden standing there with head held high like he was all that because he WAS all that. Gabby and I said hello to him and to the man on the end of Milo's leash. The man lives alone in a very small apartment and he takes Milo to Doggie Day play every day. I practically started salivating. I said, I'm getting set to be out of town for a few weeks, but if I weren't I'd offer to babysit him.

Gabby assumed a pose of great indifference a few feet away from Milo. Oh, she did a play bow and all when they first met, but then she assumed a position of great indifference, staring off in a direction that was not the direction of the dog. On the way home, I said, "Wasn't that dog handsome?????"

"He was all right," she said.

The Value of Dopey Ideas

"But is it dopey?" I asked Silvija, the wonderful woman who helps me with my garden. (Well, she doesn't "help" me. She does everything. I just admire and exclaim and occasionally say, "Wait. Is this a weed?") As for wondering if something was dopey, I was referring to a little wire cat wearing polka dot boots and a yellow sweater on which is a fish pin. It's about five to six inches tall and I got it because it was just too whimsical and cute. It sat in my basement for years, doing nothing, and then I had the idea that maybe I'd put it in the hollow of a tree outside my house, a kind of Boo Radley surprise for passersby. I opened up the cat's arms so it looked as if it were offering a hug. Later, Silvija sat the cat on a little piece of wood and added some moss on the floor of the hollow, from which grew the tiniest white flower you ever saw. People stop to look at that cat every day. My neighbor saw people taking pictures of it. And I'll bet I know what you're thinking. Why don't I take a picture of it so you can see? Two reasons. One is that, as a writer, I prefer to offer a description and let readers' imaginations come up with their own version of things. But a bigger reason is that my phone broke and I had to get a new one and I'm still trying to figure things out. Currently, when I get a text or an email, rather than getting a helpful little ping, I get a song that lasts about three hours. Or so it seems. It went off again last night when I was trying to have a conversation with Bill and I said, "I have to get that fixed," and he said, "Yeah, you have to get that fixed."
Anyway.

The wire cat reminded me that all of us have ideas that we might feel shy about, but that are probably really good ideas. On my timeline, I've been posting stories I like a lot about ideas that people had and acted on: kids who run track taking shelter dogs out with them. Little houses made for homeless vets to give them shelter and a measure of dignity. I remember my mom once going out to lunch with her three sisters, I think they were all in their eighties at the time. When they went to pay, someone had picked up their tab. That was a good idea! Immensely pleased, my mom wrote a letter to the newspaper, which was published, and so many more people got to enjoy the gesture vicariously. (I need to mention here again the time I asked FB people to send my mom a Christmas card because she so missed receiving them the way she used to. I thought she'd get 20 or so and it would be great. She received thousands. I am still so very grateful to every single one of you who gave her that miracle of kindness and care for what turned out to be her last Christmas.)

If there's any life lesson that I hope to learn better, it's the worth of giving—especially spontaneously. And I would suggest to you that there's some idea percolating inside that you kind of want to do, but worry that it might be dopey. I'm just going to go out on a limb here and say: If it's in the interest of kindness and care or whimsy that might lift someone's spirits, it's not.

In a Grocery Store Parking Lot

They say not to go to the grocery store hungry, and I almost always make sure to eat before I go to the grocery store. What good does that do? There are so many temptations in the store, from lovely asparagus stalks asking politely to be grilled after being bathed in olive oil and sprinkled lavishly with Kosher salt and freshly ground pepper, and then given a squeeze of lemon and a few gratings of Parmesan cheese. There are the nearly toxic but ever so tasty Cheetos. There are fancy cheeses galore and prosciutto sliced so thin you can read through it. Today I got some hardboiled eggs and some spicy grilled chicken from the salad bar to keep me from getting a glazed donut. I felt very virtuous as I sat in the car eating before I drove home. Across the way, I saw a man sitting on a bench outside the vet's office, the same one I go to. He was sitting very still and I thought, uh oh. I'll bet his dog is in trouble. Or his cat or his bird or his iguana. The man rested his arms on his knees and hung his head. He took off his sunglasses and wiped at his eyes. He blew his nose and then regarded the tissue as though the contents might tell his fortune. He pulled the neck of his t-shirt up to just below his eyes. He put his head down again.

I thought, I'm going to call the vet and see if he's there to have his pet put down. Or if his pet is in surgery and it doesn't look good. Or if the cost of whatever was happening was going to be an extreme hardship so I could see if I could at least anonymously make a donation toward the bill.

Just then the door of the vet's office opened and the man on the bench jumped up to go and meet another, older man, who was carrying a small dog, a kind of terrier, wrapped in a green blanket. The dog's eyes were closed. The younger man opened the front car door and got in the passenger side and reached out to receive the dog. Then he changed his mind and got in the back seat, more room, I guess. I started my car and drove toward them, wanting to say, "Are you guys okay? Anything I can do to help?" (Like what, I wondered. Telling him that the doctors at that clinic are really good? Sympathizing with them, that their pet was or had been hurting and that it hurt them, too?) As I got to behind their car, I saw that both men were sitting quietly, unable to drive quite yet, and it came to me that this moment was exquisitely private. And so I drove on, but my heart was breaking, not only because I thought the dog might be dead and was being given his final car ride before being taken home to be buried, but because of the way that so many of us love our animals so deeply and suffer so hard when they suffer.

I passed another couple of guys walking on the sidewalk and one of them had many balloons in fanciful shapes on his head. I thought he might have been entertaining children, and these balloons were the leftovers, and so the child in him was enjoying them.

I got into the area of homes and gardens and tall trees throwing dark shade, and the quiet and the beauty were comforting. Then I saw a guy leaning over to pet an old black lab; the dog's face was completely white. The dog's tail was swinging back and forth, fap, fap, fap, and seemed to keep time with the guy's patting. I looked at that dog, still alive and keeping on, and I hoped he was happy and that his man was, too. And one thing I'd bet on is that that little terrier wrapped so carefully in that green blanket, and carried so slowly across the parking lot, had had in his time many happy days.

We can be cruel and careless, we human beings. But our glory is that we can hold inside ourselves such love.

Middle-of-the-Night Reckonings

Oh, I am weary enough to do it now, die and be done with it. Or perhaps not. The ducks came back yesterday. From Robert Hillman's novel *Joyful*

Which is to say that last night, I had one of those nights. I fell asleep just fine and then awakened at 2:25am with Despair sitting over in the corner of my bedroom, leering at me. "Oh, no," I said. "Oh, goody, I woke you up," said he.

I lay there for a long time, thinking about how Bill and I have eschewed watching the news for a few days in a row, now, because both of us are filled to the brim with the seemingly insurmountable Great Divide in this country. It really is like the story of the two blind men feeling an elephant from opposite ends and describing it in ways completely different from each other.

I can't reconcile it, how it keeps going on, how it keeps getting worse. I took a walk through my wonderful neighborhood last night, and there, in the fading light, were the exuberant spring gardens: long branches of forsythia, pink and red and orange tulips still mostly closed tight and looking like so many tubes of lipstick, hyacinths that look like flower poodles, daffodils fully open and looking to me like (if you can stand another simile) little trumpet flowers wearing Elizabethan collars. Or like your most favorite and wildly exuberant aunt, welcoming you to her house, her arms thrown open wide. (I'm not quite sure why that image comes to me, but I trust you all enough to just go ahead and throw it out there. She's wearing a faded apron, too, the aunt, and there are good smells coming from her house that make their way all the way to the sidewalk.)

I saw a group of three little boys outside playing football, and their father came out and said, "Five minutes, guys," which was met with a collective groan and one little guy saying, "It's not even *dark* yet!" which was met with the father saying— you guessed it—"Five minutes."

I passed a little area on the boulevard where someone is trying to grow grass, and he put some sticks and string around it to keep dogs and people away and voila! the grass is coming. I think everyone who walks by shares in the triumph.

And yet. The daily bitterness and violence in the paper, on the news, on the streets, wears on one's soul. And then sometimes Despair comes in the night to bother you. It snatches sleep away from you as though it were ripping up a page.

But last night, I fought back. I thought of my grandchildren. I called Gabby over to pet her. (Poor Gabby, called into service when she was sound asleep and maybe dreaming of prime rib. But, dog that she is, she came over gladly, effectively rubbing her eyes and saying, "Mutt's up?" [ha ha].

Nothing was exactly working. I was getting more and more anxious. I checked my heart rate: up. I checked my Sad-O-Meter. Full. So I turned on the light and read. And Mr. Despair melted like the witch in the Wizard of Oz. I was soon smiling and laughing out loud. And guess what I was reading? A book about grammar and punctuation. But not just any book. I was reading Benjamin Dreyer's *Dreyer's English: An Utterly Correct Guide to Clarity and Style*. If you loved Strunk and White's *The Element of Style*, you'll adore this one. Who knew reading about hyphens and semicolons could draw you in so completely, to say nothing of making you LOL, as they say?

I went back to sleep soon enough, and awakened to a beautiful day, and I made myself a slice of toast and put an overly generous amount of butter and blackberry jelly on it and then I looked at puppies on line.

I am going to waste this whole day in an effort to completely mend my soul. Which is to say I'm not going to waste it at all.

Thank you for being with me here today.

Sidewalk Origami, Part I

I've been for a walk on a summer's day......

After staring at the computer screen for hours, I decide it's time for Gabby's big walk. She has stationed herself right outside my study door, and when I get up, she pops up like a jack-in-the-box and flies downstairs. She runs to get a toy to hold in her mouth while I snap on her harness because makes it makes her nervous and the toy brings her comfort, and then off we go. Past the chickens around the corner, a favorite for both of us. They are running free in their yard today and Gabby jams her nose into a corner of the fence and her tail is going a mile a minute because she and a chicken are nose to beak. So much excitement and the walk has just begun!

We pass a guy spraying something on a lawn from a tank he wears on his back. "What are you spraying?" I ask, pulling Gabby close to me. "It's for mosquitoes," he says, which does not exactly answer the question. "Did you spray it on the boulevard side, too?" I ask, because that's where I keep Gabby when I walk her. "Nah," he says, and gets in his car and drives away.

We continue on and I see two little kids sitting on the sidewalk with a box. Oh, boy, I think, a lemonade stand, and I actually have some money with me. But it is not a lemonade stand. It is an origami stand. There is a brown-haired, brown-eyed boy who is about seven years old manning the stand. He wears a striped t-shirt, shorts, and his feet are bare. He has glasses with one of those elastic holders around the back of his head. I walk up to him and he says nothing.

"Are you selling something?" I ask.

"Yes, origami," he says.

"How much is it?" I ask.

The boy: Um....I was thinking...25 cents? Or 50 cents?

Me: *I'll* give you 50 cents for an origami.

Boy: Um...I think just a quarter? And then I can start earning to buy the typewriter Lego kit from Gepetto's toy store. It's eleven dollars and change, but then I have to pay tax, too, so.....

Me: Ah yes, the tax. But I'll pay you 50 cents.

The boy looks doubtful, then allows as how maybe that would be okay. Close by is his maybe four-year-old brother, also barefoot, also in a t-shirt and shorts, but he is wearing a necklace made of very pretty beads.

Me: Do you have change for a five dollar bill?

Boy: No. I don't have any money. You're my first customer.

Me: Well, I'm going to go and get some frozen yogurt and then I'll get some change and then I can buy some origami, okay?

Boy: Okay.

Me: You know, you might want to say, when someone comes by, Would you like to buy some origami?

Boy: Yeah....

Me: It's hard, especially if you're a little shy. But you know I didn't really know you were selling it until I asked you. Also (I know, I know, who asked *me*??), maybe you could put the price on your box where it says origami for sale. And maybe raise the box up on something so people could see it?

Boy: [thinking] I *could* move it back so the tall people could see it .

Me: There you go. Okay, I'll see you in about twenty minutes, okay?

Gabby and I press on and at the end of the block I pass two women out walking. "Are you going that way?" I ask, pointing to the direction of the origami stand. "Yes," they say. I tell them about the origami stand. Word of mouth, you know.

Gabby and I cut through the park and I see that there is something placed on one of the memorial plaques there. It's a bouquet of pink roses and a stuffed rabbit wearing a tutu. The plaque is in honor of a baby who died at six weeks of age, and the words on the plaque say that the baby is *Forever in our hearts, Love Mom and Dad.* I wonder when they brought that bouquet here. I tear up a little—six weeks old! then keep walking. We go past Olive & Well, where we can buy that fabulous blueberry vinegar, we go past a guy spraying more stuff out of a tank on his back on another lawn.

"What are you spraying?" I ask. "Roundup," he says. "Does that kill birds?" I ask. He shrugs. He probably wishes I'd mind my own business. But I have been instructed to, "if I see something, say something." So I said something.

At the yogurt place, I am walking out when I hear one of the counter guys say to the other, "Did I tell you my Dad was in the circus?"

I would love to stay and eavesdrop, but I have to get back to the origami stand now that I have change.

When I arrive back at the place where the stand was, no kids are in sight. I go up to the house and ring the doorbell. The little brother comes to the door. "Sam [not real name, just in case] is in the bathroom," he says. "He's making a BM, so he told me to close up shop."

I say, "Well, should I wait?"

"Yeah!" says the amiable little brother.

I wait a couple of minutes and the little brother comes back to the door holding up his finger in that overly emphatic way kids have. "He'll be out in *one minute*," he says.

In one minute, here comes Sam, and he sits on the sidewalk and puts down his boxes, the cardboard one with stars drawn on it that says *Origami for Sale* and the wooden box where he keeps his supplies.

"Ready?" I say.

"Do you remember how much it was?" he asks.

"Well, you said 25 cents, but I'll gladly pay you 50 cents."

He looks doubtful, rolls his eyes up to consult the blue sky.

"I *think* maybe 25. But maybe 50."

"50," I say. "So what are my choices? Do you make birds?"

"Nooooooo. I'm not very good at birds. You could have a sailboat or a cup."

"Excellent," I say. "I'll take both."

"What color do you want?"

"For the boat, I'll take blue."

He considers this. "I know this guy and he *has* a sailboat, and he says he always prefers red for his boats."

"Then I'll have red."

The boy gets to work. He starts telling me about a new TV show and then looks over at his little brother, who is in the fenced-in yard beside him bouncing up and down on a big ball and singing a little song in a high, soft voice.

"My brother," he says, "or—I mean, my assistant—is supposed to talk to the customer. I make the origami and make change. He talks to the customer and hands them their origami. But...." he looks over at his brother. "He's taking a break."

"That's okay," I say.

He makes the sailboat and then he wants to know what color I want for the cup.

"Blue," I say.

"Good," he says. "That color is on top. You can't drink out of this. It's really just for....."

"Paper clips?" I ask helpfully.

"Snacks," he says. "It's actually quite useful."

He completes it and hands it to me, demonstrating how you just stick your fingers in and voila! a cup.

"This is great!" I say. "Thank you."

"You're welcome," he says.

Another potential customer is coming down the street. I wish Sam would leap up and say, "Hey, Mister, would you like to buy some origami?" But I'm pretty sure he won't. I'm pretty sure he'll just sit there. But you know, maybe he's right. He's a dollar closer to that Lego typewriter.

Chickens + Grandson = Joy

Many of you know I love chickens. All of you know I love my grandchildren. So when I got this photo of my grandson from my daughter....

Sidewalk Origami, Part II

Out for a walk with Gabby, which will include our eating lunch together at our favorite outdoor cafe. At the cafe, she lies under the table in the shade, I sit in a chair and feed her scraps. She has water in a tin foil dish, I have iced tea. She is so good, people don't even know she's there, which they always tell me on our way out. "Oh, my goodness!" they say. "I didn't even know she was there, she was so good!" "Thank you," I say. Once we're down the block, Gabby always calls me on that. "I don't know why you say thank you when the compliment is clearly meant for me," she says, and I say, "I do that on your behalf, because you can't talk." And she says, "Oh, really? Isn't my language in the ear of the beholder? What am I doing right now, playing tiddlywinks?"

Anyway, today we're walking down the block toward the restaurant, and there it is, the origami stand I visited yesterday.

"How's business?" I ask Sam, the proprietor, who sits on the sidewalk behind his origami supply box with legs crossed like a Yogi.

"Good!" he says. It looks like Sam is helping with the economy, because he has apparently hired more kids to be out there with him today. There is a really pretty little girl about his age who tells me her name is Emily. [I never use real kids' names, by the way, just to protect them.] I tell her my name and Gabby's. The other kid is a little guy, about four, wearing glasses and a big Band-Aid over one eye, and the Band-Aid's whimsical design makes me think he's being treated for strabismus. His name is Perry, and I believe he is Emily's brother.

"Do you guys have a dog?" I ask.

"No," Emily says. "We can't have a dog because my dad is allergic."

"Nuh uh!" says Sam. "It's because Perry's *afraid* of dogs!"

Perry takes a big step forward, quickly, as though to defend himself, but then he seems to realize that Sam is only speaking the truth and so he steps back without saying anything. Would that we all could admit defeat so gracefully, without defensive posturing or retaliatory rhetoric.

"I think I need another cup," I tell Sam the origami man. "A friend saw the one you made me yesterday and she wants one, too." A lie, but a white one.

"Okay," Sam says. He stands. "Buuuuuuut you could have *two*, if you have a dollar!"

Well. Look who's gone to the Wharton School of Business overnight.

"Let me see if I have a dollar," I say. I know I have a dollar, but I want to prolong the suspense.

I slowly take out my wallet. Slowly take a peek. "I do have a dollar!" I say, and he does that kind of happy kid jump where they don't really jump but just bend their knees like they're going to. I think I do it, too.

Emily helps with color selection, and we decide on orange and yellow, happy citrus colors. Then, while Sam makes the origami, Emily chats me up, which is what Sam's brother was supposed to do yesterday, but he didn't. (See earlier post about Sam's brother's "break.") Keeping with the theme of pets (always a good idea to stay with the subject your customer introduced), Emily tells me that her Nana gave her two frogs, but one died because the other one bit its arm off.

"No!" I say.

"Yeah," she says, in a regretful but resigned tone. "And then the other one just died of I don't know what."

"I'm sorry," I say.

"Then we had some fish," she says, and I know what's coming next. Yup. They died.

By now, my cups are ready. I hand over the dollar, and say, "Well, good luck, I hope you reach your goal soon and can buy that Lego typewriter."

"I will!" he says. "Because of you I only need one dollar more!"

Well, it's because of *him*, but....You know. Learn to take a compliment, even if it's misplaced. (Gabby: Yeah, you know a lot about that.)

Sam then tells me the toy he wants is a storm trooper. "And I never had a Lego storm trooper," he said.

"I thought it was a typewriter!" I say.

"It's a storm trooper who comes *with* a typewriter," he says.

Ah. A Renaissance man. I would like to meet a storm trooper with a typewriter. I would like to go out to lunch with him. I would like to go out to dinner with him.

I have to tell you one more thing. As I was leaving, and about halfway down the block, I heard a little voice call out, "Goodbyyyyyyye, honey!" It think it was Perry. There was some giggling. Then he said it again, louder, "GOODBYE, HONEY!!!!" and there was much convulsive laughter. It made me wish I was a kid and could fall down in the grass and laugh with them.

But going out to lunch with Gabby is good, too.

Gabby: *Thank* you.

Solar Eclipse

There seemed to be two distinct schools of thought regarding the eclipse today: those who thought it was exciting, magical, a *must see*, and those who were awfully indifferent. I fell into the latter category, and I'm not sure why. Usually I love things like this, demonstrations of the mightiness of nature. Not this time. Well, not this time except until about 12:30 this afternoon. The eclipse was supposed to start happening at 1:00. So I raced home from running errands, wondering how I could possibly not have cared about this event. The sky would darken, and it would appear that night had fallen. And then the sun would come again. Simple words, but a profound feeling associated with them. It was kind of like the nature video I watched this morning of wolves howling, which gave me chills. It was that sense of something primordial and, although mysterious, bound up with elemental truths that we might not be able to articulate but know in our bones. I thought of how someone who was ignorant of eclipses might have viewed it, maybe someone long, long ago. He comes out of his cave, swinging his club, on his way to work. The sun is out, the day is fine. Suddenly, the sky darkens, blackens, the temperature drops, the birds silence, and the man's heart is full of fear. He waits for doomsday, he waits for he doesn't know what. But then all returns to normal. He realizes he's here. He realizes what he has. He goes back to the cave, and his partner is at the entrance, her eyes wide. "Did you....?" he asks, in caveman language, and she nods in the universal and time-less language. They stare at each other like they've never seen each other before. And they embrace. And then he shrugs, and goes to work, his club swinging at his side.

What does it take for us to know our great luck at being here and alive? What suggests the benevolence of the mighty forces around us? Maybe a total eclipse of the sun. And maybe the caveman took in it all in stride because in those days, the world was so *full* of miracles.

Then again, it still is.

Comfort Food

I need a break from the devastating news; therefore, I'm going to give you a really good pasta recipe.

Bow Tie Pasta with Sausage, Tomato and Cream (aka "Pink Pasta")

Heat 2 T. olive oil in large skillet. Add 1 lb. sweet Italian sausage (I used chicken sausage) and 1/2 t. dried red pepper flakes, breaking sausage into small bits. Cook until no longer pink. Add 1 medium chopped onion and 3 cloves minced garlic, cook another 5 minutes or so. Add one 28-oz can Italian plum tomatoes, drained and coarsely chopped, 1-1/2 cups whipping cream (or evaporated milk or half and half) and a little salt. Cook on low to medium heat until mixture thickens, about 4-5 minutes.

Serve over cooked bow tie pasta or ziti. Sprinkle with freshly grated Parmesan cheese and a bit of chopped parsley.

This tastes way better than the recipe suggests!!

Recipe given to me by Laura Hays.

It's a Wonderful World

If there's one thing I love, it's driving through the country. Yesterday, on stop number two for the "Tales and Tails Tour," we drove to Morenci, Michigan, population 2,220. On the way there, I saw rolling green hills, which never fail to move me. I saw waving wheat, two white butterflies chasing each other, mile after mile of purple wildflowers, red barns, white barns, blue barns, and, at one place, a family of barns: two big ones side by side, and a very small one off to the side. I saw a field full of white cows. In a pasture of standing horses, I saw one suddenly lie down—WHOOMPH!—and he looked very pleased with himself. I saw a pen full of goats, with a tire in there that they seemed to be playing with. I saw acres of corn, backlit by the sun. I saw twin palominos that I really, really wanted. At the intersection of two county roads, I saw a large stand of Queen Anne's lace, that most underrated of blossoms. I saw a line of birds on the wire, gossiping together in their open-air cafe. I saw the melancholy trailing branches of a willow tree. There was a huge field of sunflowers which I so regret not getting a picture of, there were trailer parks, there were cattails growing next to ponds. You get in a certain mindset, driving on roads like this, or at least I do. I get peaceful. And so funny: you leave a city where there are eight lanes of traffic to drive on a two-lane highway, and you get so used to it in such a short period of time that things like this happen: After driving and driving and driving, we came to something that made Bill say: "Wow! A traffic light!"

Come. Gather. Eat.

Bill, Gabby and I have been on the road touring for "Tales and Tails." It has been exhilarating, but also tiring. So it was that when we were early for one event, I suggested we find some cool green space and take a nap in the car. Bill said, "You take a nap, I'll take Gabby for a walk." There are many differences between Bill and me and here is one of them: I need at least eight hours of sleep at night or I feel like a rope unraveling; he seemingly needs no sleep. But never mind, that was a wonderful offer he made me, and we found a little park and I immediately fell into a peaceful sleep. I was awakened by the sound of a kid yelling, "Hike!" and I opened my eyes to see a group of boys around ten or twelve years old playing football. Never mind that their field was about the size of a card table, they played in earnest. Well, all except the kid who appeared bored, and, rather than attending to the action of the game, he was doing that old dance move in the Charleston where you put your hands over your kneecaps and move your legs in and out and it looks like your knees are changing places with each other. (That was me as a kid, hopeless at any sport, and so I always needed an alternative activity. Usually it was daydreaming or sucking on the ends of my braids, but if it was baseball and I was in the outfield, I made dandelion bouquets.) I heard a kid say, "Guys! Guys!" which is the kid clarion call for putting a motion on the table. The kid said something and they all took off running like a herd of pony people.

Here came the adults, and then, a musician setting up his sound system, saying, "Check. Check. Check." Grills were being prepared for cooking. I hoped they were having hamburgers and hot dogs and marshmallows. Is there anything better than toasted marshmallows or a little-bit-burned weenie off the grill? The women began to lay the tables, and at least one of them was wearing an apron, which thrilled me. I thought, oh, I hope they have pastel mixing bowls full of macaroni salad and potato salad and a crock of homemade baked beans. I hope they have pies and cakes the ladies made and thick watermelon slices. I thought, I'll bet if you asked every man, woman and child in this park if they are happy right now, they'd laugh and say, "Well...Yes! Of course!"

The waning of summer. The joy of a picnic. The license to run around hollering and making up games, and using your t-shirt to wipe your mouth and nobody says not to.

The crack of a bat, children tearing around yelling or sitting grouped beneath the shade of a tree splitting blades of grass and sharing quieter kid talk, a tablecloth snapping in the breeze before the women lay it on the table and smooth it down with their hands and maybe weight it with rocks. Men gathered around the grill with a spatula in one hand and a bottle of beer in the other. These are the sights and sounds of my childhood and I am so relieved to see they are still here, those things that say Come. Gather. Eat. It's one more nice day and we're all right here.

Simple Acts of Kindness

I was talking to someone the other day about the level of anxiety and despair that exists now, the way that most of us are preoccupied with trying to grapple with all that is happening. It's funny, but a scene I recently witnessed at the library seemed to encapsulate a lot of things for me. A large-sized, large-voiced African American woman, let's call her Ann, was sitting on a window ledge next to a small-ish dark haired young white woman. Ann was saying, "So she says, you need blah blah blah, and I'm thinking what *is* that? And then she says you have to blah blah blah, and I'm thinking, what is *that*? And she says you are blah blah blah and so here is the blah blah blah, what *is that*?"

I thought, I kind of don't know what you're saying, yet I think I'm right with you. I wanted to walk up to her and say, "How about we go on over to George's Diner and have some breakfast together? And we can toast each other with our coffee mugs and say, This? This is good coffee. And then we can bang our muffins together and say, These? These are good muffins and inside them are many lovely blueberries." We could have just seen eye to eye, literally, we could have lost ourselves in the lovely necessity of a meal. We could have reminded ourselves that in all this swirling chaos there is the comfort of company and conversation and coffee. This is what people can do for each other, anytime, anywhere, they can ground each other, celebrate each other, and remind each other of life's great worth, even in the midst of such horrors as so many are experiencing now. Last night, on TV, I watched people sitting in a shelter, and I felt so bad for them. But also I was thinking, I'll bet there will be almost no smallness of heart on display in that shelter, no meanness of spirit. I'll bet they are going to take care of one another. And although they are suffering now, and although great and lingering hardships lie ahead, they will at least have seen up close and personal how we really are all in this together, and how one thing never changes: we all rely on our heart and humanity and simple acts of kindness to get us through.

Books

I read today that a publisher despaired of the sales of books and attributed it to a sense of distraction. I know that many of us are sensitive to the mood of the nation, which of late has not been good, and that we all hurt for the people of Houston and Bangladesh. But this is not a time to be distracted. This is a time to pay attention and to try to make things as right as we can, by compassionate outreach near and far. As for reading, I don't know of anything that works better to soothe an aching heart than getting lost in a story. I find that books pull me out of despair. They educate, enlighten, and entertain. They remind me of the many things that connect us, the things that matter, the things that endure. They also remind me of the need for contemplation and reflection and stillness. Try to find at least half an hour a day to read, and see if it doesn't help you. If you have a dog sleeping beside you, even better. Or a cat in your lap. Or birds singing outside. Or a sunset or sunrise happening, or coffee brewing, or a cake baking or a chicken roasting.

Once again you can see my love of domestics forcing its way in. On a certain kind of day, I even like scouring the bathtub. Why I never took Home Ec in high school is beyond me. Hey, that reminds me: cookbooks are also good to read. My favorite cookbook authors are Ann Hodgman and Ruth Reichl. Delicious literature, you might say.

Long Flight Delay

On my way home from Traverse City, I got to the airport early. I thought it was going to be about forty minutes early but whoops! it turned out to be five hours early. Yup. Yet another looooooong delay in a smaaaalllll airport. What to do.

Well, read, of course.

Eat, of course.

And eavesdrop.

Behind me was a gentleman about my age talking to a woman who was on the same flight as we were. She was from Traverse City, so she gave up and went home, saying she might as well just come back later. So the gentleman, let's call him Ron, and I began to talk. I opened with, "I heard you talking about hunting dogs. Do you like dogs?"

Well.

Cut to an hour and a half later. We had nearly exhausted ourselves showing each other photos of dogs. I showed Ron the dog I'm going to look at on Thursday and his eyes grew misty. "I'll tell you what," he said. "I'd take ever' one of those dogs at the rescue. And my wife, she would too. She always wants the first one jumps up when it sees her. And then she wants all the rest."

"I *know*," I said.

The guy and I watched each others' suitcases so that we could each wander off unencumbered to the bathroom, to the restaurant. When I was at the counter of the restaurant, two guys from England came in and surveyed the menu. "What's a Sloppy *Joe*?" one of them asked, wrinkling his nose. The young woman behind the counter had a little difficulty explaining it to him. "It's...you know, ground beef...." she began and then she kind of ran out of gas. Her co-worked rushed to the rescue to add, "And it has tomato sauce!"

Now, you know and I know that a Sloppy Joe—a good Sloppy Joe—has far more than that. So I had to add my two cents and I said, "They're a little spicy and they're really good!"

"Well, I'll have one," said one of the men and then the other said, "Me, too," and I felt very satisfied. I started to sit down and eat my turkey sandwich and suddenly I got nervous. I went back to the counter where the men were waiting for their meal and I said, "What if you don't like them? Then I'll feel guilty." "Ah, don't worry," they said. After I finished my sandwich, I passed by the men's table. Their plates, I was relieved to see, could qualify for the Clean Plate Club. "*So????*" I asked, and the one man smiled and the other said, "Very nice."

I went back out to talk about dogs some more with Ron and asked if he had gotten his baggage tag because this was a small plane and we'd have to gate-check. Proudly, he showed me what he'd put on his bag, but it was just the ID tag: name, address. I went and got him the right tag and I felt like Big Mama of the Airport.

"Want to see that dog I'm going to look at again?" I asked.

"Yup," he said.

Then we talked about his time in Viet Nam. The pain was still there, that's for sure.

Then we talked about books.

Then the lady who had gone home came back and we acted like it was old home week.

That loooonnng delay? It was actually nice. Because we all slowed down. We all were friendly with each other. And we all took care of one another. In a nutso world, it's nice to see such civility.

Gabby here: Elizabeth is *obsessed* with that dog. She might need a little tiny reminder that if I don't like him, all bets are off. He's half Australian Shepherd, half standard poodle. He probably wears an ascot when he chases sheep around. Elizabeth showed me his photo. He's all right. He's reallly shaggy. If I get a vote, his name is Wookie.

New Puppy Chronicles

Guess who's here?

We've settled on Austin for a name for him, at least for now, because it was one Bill and I both agreed on. He has learned to go up and down stairs like a champ. He loves Gabby. With the exception of one mistake, he's relieved himself outside.

I have a plaster of Paris pig on the floor of the dining room. Austin is not sure what to make of him. He growled at him a little, just to show who's boss.

Gabby: Who are you barking at?

Austin: This here pig! I've seen these fellers before, down in Mississippi, where I came from. You gotta keep an eye on them.

Gabby: The pig is not real.

Austin: Say what?

Gabby: The pig is not real.

Austin: Well....You can't be too careful.

Austin also barked at those little humans on the TV screen. Otherwise, he's been quite the gent. He likes to admire himself in the floor length mirror and make a pile of toys and then lie on top of it.

Up at five AM, though. Remember those puppy days?

His name should really be Rags, because he looks like a pile of them.

Austin, the new puppy: Whew, I'm 'bout to blow a gasket. I went on a long walk which was as much fun as making a coon dog cross-eyed. I made a lot of friends. I wouldn't be surprised if I get elected mayor of this town. Now I'm taking a nap, as you can see. I look like I'm dead to the world, but let me tell you: All that has to happen is for Elizabeth to make a move and I'll be up like the first kernel of popped corn.

Gabby the Golden, senior dog of the household: Mayor. Right. He IS growing on me, though. I like to take toys away from him. Builds character. And I'm glad to have someone to talk to when Elizabeth and Bill go out. Austin's choice of subject matter is a bit limited, however, as he likes to talk about himself and himself alone.

"Who do you like for 2020?" I asked him last night. "Me," he said. Actually, he beats out some of the candidates I know.

Five a.m., and Austin's up. Then Gabby's up because Austin's up. Then I'm up because Gabby and Austin are up.

I am *tired*. My face looks like an asterisk. (I think I've heard that elsewhere, but I don't know where and therefore cannot provide proper accreditation. Sorry.) But my face does look like an asterisk, all creased and puffy and unsure as to what direction it wants to go in terms of expression.

But I pad downstairs and let the dogs out. Let the dogs in. Feed them. I have never seen a dog eat so fast as Austin. I might rename him Hoover. I have never seen a dog attempt to eat everything that looks remotely edible (to him) on every walk that he takes: leaves, sticks, wood chips. He licks any remnant of anything stuck onto the sidewalk—or at least tries to. My vocabulary lately consists of two phrases: "Leave it" and "Drop it." Oh, and, because sometimes he attacks Gabby to play with her before she's ready, "Leave her alone, not yet."

But look at him, I tell myself, his coat looks like a dandelion gone to seed, with all those long hairs sticking up. His eyes are full of nothing but joy. For him, waking is stepping up to the Big Buffet: food, toys, affection and play, and he just can't wait to have at it all. Thank goodness, he is also a wonderful napper, after he has been going 100 miles an hour for a while.

I took a walk with the dogs after they ate break-fast, and my weariness began to fade, to kind of burn off like morning fog. The bright-colored flowers in gardens, upright or leaning. The empty playground, some little rain boots forgotten and left at a fence's edge for reclaiming. The grass still wet with dew, the air cool. A car passes occasionally, and I wonder where the drivers are going. To work? If I had to get up this early to go to work, I'd want it to be at a bakery, where I would walk in the door and be greeted by sugar and butter.

When I come home, I make coffee and then Bill comes down and we read the papers. Well, he only tries to read the paper because I keep interrupting with stories that I think he must hear about right away. "I know you're trying to read," I say, and he always says, "Go ahead." Today, one of my interruptions was about the author Ocean Vuong. I'm so excited to read his book *On Earth We're Briefly Gorgeous.* That's what I'll read after I finish the absolutely lovely *Henry, Himself* by Stewart O'Nan.

Well, a breakfast of bagels and lox. The sun rises higher in the sky. Next door, they're getting the grill ready for a good workout today. We too have laid in a supply of things to grill: sausages, onions, peppers, corn on the cob, cauliflower steaks, and I'll make a sweet corn gazpacho that I originally tried because it had such an odd ingredient in it: green grapes.

Sweet Corn Gazpacho
Serves 6

1 lb. yellow tomatoes, roughly chopped
1 yellow bell pepper, seeded and roughly chopped
3 ears of sweet corn, kernels removed from cob
1/4 c. sweet white onion, roughly chopped
1/2 c. green seedless grapes
1 Persian cucumber, peeled and chopped
2 small garlic cloves, smashed
1/2 jalapeño pepper, seeded
Sea salt
1/4 c. olive oil
1 T. white balsamic vinegar
1 lime, juiced
Optional: hot sauce, chive oil

1. Combine the tomatoes, bell pepper, corn, onion, grapes, cucumber, garlic, and jalapeño in a large bowl. Sprinkle with 1 tsp. of sea salt, mix well, and set the bowl aside for one hour, covered.

2. Put the mixture in a blender with the olive oil and blend until it reaches your desired smoothness. Stir in the vinegar and lime juice, then season to taste with sea salt. Serve lightly chilled; pretty it up with a hot sauce or chive oil garnish.

From *House Beautiful.*

Austin has had three walks so far today, and it's only 9:52. For this last one, I called him to put on his leash and he looked at me like, "Oy. Are you kidding?" Still, he followed resolutely, picking up leaves and sticks and everything else he found but quickly dropping them. This is our compromise. I let him pick things up; he immediately drops them. And we didn't even have to go to couples counseling to come to this arrangement.

Now, he lies snoring on the floor of my office. I wish I could record it and put it on here, it's so cute and ruffly sounding. A person probably can do such things, but not this person This person had acute anxiety when hotel keys changed from slide-in to hover-over. And don't even get me started on the alarm clocks they have in hotel rooms now. They alarm me all right, because I have no idea how to work them. Apparently one is meant to (or can) use one's device to wake up to one's playlist. (That sentence is full of vocabulary that makes me nervous.) Here's how I like to wake up: [Knock Knock!] Room service! And after the meal is wheeled in: "May I pour you a cup of coffee?"

How come when Austin snores, I find it adorable, but when Bill snores, I want to murder him?

Gabby is tolerating Austin, and seems to enjoy playing with him, but she needs her breaks. She looks up imploringly at me, and that's when I know to give her a copy of Bark magazine and a tall cool one (i.e. a drink of water) and put her in the living room, a gate between her and Mr. Red Bull.

What *is* he?

Three weeks into my relationship with Mr. Pups (Austin). His eyes have changed from a kind of general friendly willingness to warm recognition. The bond is here, and growing. Gabby now looks for him first thing for her morning exercise routine (talk about your downward dogs!) and Bill and I leave the kitchen door propped open so that we can watch Austin occasionally burst into the kitchen, race around the island, and then gallop back outside. Out on the deck, Gabby stands watching as he does this. When he gets back to her, she says, "Great moves, pal," and then grabs him and flings him to the ground, after which he gets up and manages to get under her where she can't reach him.

Yesterday, I took both dogs for a car ride. Austin came into places so that he could get used to the fact that the world is varied and mostly kind. At the hardware store, the cashier gave him a biscuit and asked the question everyone asks when they see him: What kind of a dog *is* that? "Ask his honky-tonk mother," is what I want to say but instead I dutifully inform anyone who asks that I was told he was Aussie and Standard Poodle. Then, inevitably, people weigh in with what *they* think is in him. Here are some guesses I've heard: St. Bernard. Great Pyrenees, Irish Wolfhound, Airedale. I can hardly wait to ride him to Trader Joe's.

He went to the Town Hall so that I could get a parking sticker. A woman there came charging out of her office and made a bee line for Austin and pet him, saying, "Aren't you cute? Aren't you *cute*! Do you want to come home with me?" Then she had a question for me. Can you guess what the question was?

I took him last to pick up some cushions I had made. In the upholstery store, I asked the man if it was okay if Austin was in there. The man eyed him suspiciously. "He's house-trained," I said. Which he is. Mostly. "Okay, then," the guy said, and then after he handed me my cushions, he said, "What kind of a dog *is* that?" I told him. The man knew better. "That dog's got husky in him," he said.

Whatever. Gabby, Austin and I all came home and had lunch.

It was a good day.

Austin's doing well, loves everyone, except for the woman in the take-out window at McDonald's who handed us our food. He growled at her. I think he couldn't figure out what the heck she *was*, or else he was disapproving of our choice of cuisine, and if so, he was absolutely right. But we were tired and hungry and that's when we really like junk food.

When we got home, I put Austin in the crate so I could take a nap (see earlier note on him awakening at five) and he howled like I'd shut the door on his tail, which I most assuredly had not. He probably knows I hate crating dogs, even though most of them seem to like it. Anyway, I brought him into my office and he promptly fell asleep, which is what I'm going to do, too. I guess I'll join him on the office floor.

Today he got a harness and a most beguiling bone-shaped name tag and some toys for his crate (which we will *have* to use sometimes) and a toy chicken and some bath sheets because he can't yet have a bath and he reeks of the shelter. Don't tell him I said that.

Austin: I heard that. You know, *you* wear perfume, which, EW.

Gabby: Don't talk bad about my mom.

Austin: Okay. Whatever you say, boss.

Gabby: If someone's going to talk bad about my mom, it'll be me, not you.

Austin: Got it. Want to play with my chicken?

Conversation on the Front Porch with Austin

Austin lies casually beside the climbing hydrangea bush, chomping on the leaves.

Me: Hey, Austin?

Austin: Yeah?

Me: May I see you for a moment?

Austin: Ummmm.......

Me: Austin. Come.

Austin: Ummmmmmmm....

Me: [Pulling leaves from his mouth.] Do you see these?

Austin: Yeah. I mean, I just put them in my mouth, so I saw them. Good leaves. Good front porch party! I can't decide what's better, barking at dogs and people going down the sidewalk or eating leaves.

Me: Yeah, well, both those things are forbidden.

Austin: For*bidden*?

Me: [Showing him leaves.] These are leaves. You cannot eat them. They can make you sick. [Handing him chew toy.] You can have this.

Austin: I already played with that.

Me: Play with it again.

Austin: Geez.

Me: That's right. And quit barking at people.

Austin: I'm just telling them things they need to know. And Gabby barks too.

Me: This is not Gabby's time to be disciplined. This is your time to be disciplined.

Austin: I like when I just get pet.

Me: I know you do. Come here and I'll pet you for not eating leaves any more.

Austin: Ever?

Me: Ever.

Austin: How about for now?

Me: [Sighs]

Austin: Okay, okay. Look, see? I'm chewing my boring-I've-already-done-it chew toy that tastes of saliva instead of these interesting leaves with notes of oak and pepper and berry. And a long, smooth finish.

Me: Well, aren't you the cosmopolitan?

Austin: Yeah. You should name me Cosmo.

Me: I should name you Conniver.

Austin: Too many syllables. Let's go for a walk.

Me: I'm *trying* to read the paper.

Austin: Too many syllables. Plus it puts you in a bad mood. Come on. Let's go find butterflies.

Me: Okay. Come on, Gabby.

Gabby: You do everything he says.

Gabby Talks

Gabby: May I see you for a moment? In private? Which is a way I hardly ever see you any more?

Me: Of course! [We seclude ourselves in my office. I sit on my chair. Gabby sits before me.]

Gabby: I want to talk to you about Charlie Wanker.

Me: ....Who?

Gabby: Charlie Wanker.

Me: Who's that?

Gabby: *You* call him "Austin."

Me: Why do you call him Charlie Wanker?

Gabby: Because he's a [affecting English accent] wanker.

Me: I'm not sure....Do you know what "wanker" means?

Gabby: [Sticking with accent.] Indeed I do. A wanker is a person who...pleasures himself. Also the term also means a person who is disreputable. Both definitions apply here. You have seen Austin trying to sit on my head and...well, hump me, have you not?

Me: I stop him when he does that.

Gabby: Yes, but what about all the times he comes slamming into me and starts chewing at my underbelly or hanging from the fur 'round my neck? It's bloody awful.

Me: You're going to have to get rid of that accent if you want to have a serious discussion.

Gabby: Fine.

Me: So, remember when I asked the vet about him bothering you? And the vet said you'd let him know if it got to be too much?

Gabby: Remember when you told your FB friends I would never do that because I'm too gentle?

Me: Yes. It's true. I never see you growl at him or bite him. Although sometimes, in play, you do kind of body slam him.

Gabby: *Completely deserved.*

Me: I agree.

Gabby: I have circles under my eyes because of him getting up at the ungodly hour of 5:30 every morning.

Me: Me, too.

Gabby: We're not talking about you right now.

Me: So.....is it too much for you, having a puppy? Even if we take care to try to separate you when necessary?

Gabby: It is a bit much. I'm eight, you know. I have the gray starting on my face.

Me: I know, sweetheart. You know you're number one dog, right?

Gabby: Well, I'd *thought* so.

Me: Do you feel Austin has replaced you in our affections?

Gabby: Well, not replaced. But he has moved into your affections. And if I may add, that dog has gas sometimes that practically peels the paint off the walls.

Me: True. I had a golden named Toby who had that problem. One time I was being interviewed by a newspaper person who'd come to the house and Toby made the air practically unbreathable.

Gabby: We're not talking about Toby now.

Me: Right. So....What do you want me to do? Is he really making your life miserable?

Gabby: I have to say that sometimes that's true. You'll notice I sometimes lie in the corner and sulk?

Me: Do you ....Oh dear. Do you want me to rehome him?

Gabby: [sighs] No, he'll grow out of it. He doesn't try to attack me when we go out for walks anymore.

Me: Right! See?

Gabby: But the thing is, I'm not going to call him Austin. I'm going to call him Charlie Wanker. Okay?

Me: Okay. But what's with the Charlie?

Gabby: It's less rude if I put Charlie in front of Wanker. I don't want to be too terribly mean. I'm a gentle dog. A sweet girl.

Me: You are, and I love you so much. Everybody who meets you loves you.

Gabby: It's true, isn't it?

Me: Yup. And just remember, when we do the Michigan tour in August, you'll have a whole week without him.

Gabby: Wait. What do you mean? He's not coming?

Me: He's not coming.

Gabby: Well. Well. I'm not sure I like that.

Me: We'll bring him back a nice present, okay?

Gabby: [silence]

Me: You'll have more room in the car, and all the attention of Bill and me and everyone who comes to the readings.

Gabby: I guess when you put it that way...And I'll tell you what. I feel so much better having vented, I'll call him Austin.

Austin: [from downstairs] Hello? Gabby? Did you call me? Hey, Gabby! Gabby! Want to play with the stuffed animals? The ball? Want to just wrestle?

Gabby: [sighs] Give a girl a cookie?

Me: You got it. Two.

The Ultimate Quilt

Why is it that when I'm about to leave for the airport, everything around my house seems so precious? My favorite blue coffee mug, my embroidered pillowcase, and, needless to say, my dog? *And* the little book of Emily Dickinson letters that I read from every day?

I give you her on snow: *"I come in descending flakes, dear Dr. Holland, for verily it snows, and as descending swans, here a pinion and there a pinion, and anon a plume, come the bright inhabitants of the white home. I know they fall in Springfield; perhaps you see them now—and therefore I look out again, to see if you are looking."*

Words. The ultimate quilt.

Oh Christmas Tree, Oh Christmas Tree

One year, I did nothing to decorate my house for the holidays. I thought, oh, who cares? There are beautiful decorations all over the place; I'll just enjoy someone else's labor and creativity. Cut to this year, when I went a little nuts. I am not a talented decorator. I am a tacky decorator. But Christmas doesn't care. Christmas is an enabler. Hang those dog ornaments! it says. Bring on the glitter! Put up those poorly sewn stockings you made and wait for them to be filled!

I even got a second Christmas tree for my bedroom. I'd been sick and feeling a little sorry for myself (I'm *fine* now!) and I thought to wake up to a lighted tree would be good medicine and I was right. Beneath that bedroom tree are beautifully wrapped boxes, all empty. I just like the look of the wrapped gifts, that's why I did it.

Or so I thought.

What I've begun to do, though, is to imagine what might be in there if they *did* hold gifts. And this prompted a rush of imagination. I've thought not only of what could be in there, but what was in boxes similar in size over the years. And *that* prompted a rush of nostalgia. I thought of the gifts I loved most getting over the years: my Ginny doll outfits, my teddy bear that I named Hope, the ring with my initials, my soft gray sweater that I got as a senior in high school and found so beautiful I took it in my room and just held it. The Chanel No. 5 perfume my grandmother sent me when I was fourteen and I thought it was unbearably sophisticated to wear it.

The Joy of Cooking, which I got one year—my first non-kid cookbook. I thought of gifts that others got: the year my mom got a white mink coat which she never, ever, ever wanted, it was my Dad who wanted to give one to her. She modeled it that Christmas and then never much wore it again. It hung in the closet asking the other coats, "What'd I do? Did I do something wrong?" That gift was not as bad as the dead butterfly tray I made for her one year, and then there was the really tacky candle I tried to make for my poor brother, who, upon opening it, just gave me a look.

Then, looking at the boxes, I started having memories: the time our dog Sassy ate the assortment of gift cheeses under the tree and tried to drink train oil, for example.

I think I'll hold to keeping those empty wrapped boxes up in my bedroom every year. And because of them I'll see my cousins and me in the playroom of our grandparent's house, tearing around and screaming bloody murder while the grownups finished making the gravy and laying the table. I'll see my mom on her last Christmas, when my sister and I huddled with her in her living room, the three of us opening our gifts to each other. Our real gift? We were all still here.

As we all are still here. Aren't we lucky. We are.

Happy holidays to everyone. Enjoy the gift of your imaginations.

Love you guys, most sincerely.

Valentine Tree

The year-round Christmas tree in my bedroom is covered with valentines, including my favorite, homemade ones. I am terrible at making them, but as my friend Phyllis taught me, a homemade valentine is always great. I rely quite a bit on glitter. I cannot tell you what cheer this tree brings me, especially here in the otherwise great city of Chicago, which goes gray most of the winter.

Last night I lay in bed reading, and it was slow going, because I kept looking over at the tree. "Oh, hi," I said, once, with the kind of thrilled affection one normally shows, oh, say, a grandchild. And it said, "Hey. How you doing?" This though it already knew the answer, which was that I was happy as can be, because of the warmth of little lights in the dark.

Thanksgiving

The night before last, I stayed awake until around
four a.m., worrying about my friends in California
suffering from the bad air caused by the devastating
fires. When I spoke with them the next day, one was
making an elaborate birthday card, and she said
jokingly, "These things don't make themselves, you
know!" Then she was going out to celebrate her and
her husband's fortieth anniversary.

The other friend had just gone to get all the
things she needed to prepare Thanksgiving dinner.
She said, "I feel like Nero." She also said someone
else was doing the pies. She said, "If I do pies, I'll go
down the pie rabbit hole and never get anything else
done." I know what she means. She makes pies that
not only are delicious, but are elaborately decorated
works of art.

So there my friends are, alive and still very
much themselves, and if they need anything, it's not
my worry over them, but my love for them.

The other day I said before an audience that
being a nurse taught me that it never helps to bring
someone in a tough situation your own sorrow; they
have enough of their own. I ought to listen to myself.

Let us never fail to acknowledge the sorrow
and the problems in the world, and let us always
work against such things; but let us make sure that
what we love and what sustains us is also
acknowledged.

A Visit to the Vet

For two days, Gabby has had more matter than usual in her left eye. Today, I see that it has become what I think is conjunctivitis. Our vet is not available due to computer problems (!!) but we are directed to another clinic about twenty minutes away. We're a little nervous, because we love our vet—and the Gabester—so much, and you never know.... Upon entering the office, we see a black and white snout sticking out from under a door with a high-cut bottom. "Who's that?" I ask. "That little trouble maker?" asks the receptionist. "I thought I was the trouble maker," says Bill. "Well, he's another one," the receptionist says. "That's Tater Tot, he belongs to one of the doctors. Now, your baby Gabby will be seen when the baby ahead of her comes out of the room."

Okay. We take a seat on the bench. Gabby jumps up on the seat and sits close beside me. "I'm not a bit nervous," she tells me. "I just know you are." A white dog with well-placed black spots that make him look like he could have starred in an episode of *The Little Rascals* comes in. This is Snow, as it happens. He lies down and quietly begins panting, staring steadily ahead. Next Champ comes in, or is assisted in. He's a very old dog, and his hind legs kind of quit on him today. When he tries to get up, not much happens, but after he's given an assist by his loving owner, he sits proud as can be, ears erect. Next a little guy, one of those who always look like they just came from the beauty parlor waltzes in. As the owner talks to the receptionist, he surveys the crowd. Gabby offers a half howl, half woof comment. A dog named Kiki comes in and sits next to her and now I can see Gabby trying to come up with topics for conversation. "Come here often?" "Do you belong to Bark Box?"

I tell Champ's owners that when Homer couldn't get up on his own anymore, we got a very handy devise with a handle that effectively turned Homer into a really cute suitcase. "Yeah, my mom was just texting me about that," the guy says. He's such a nice man, and his wife is also so very kind, she has eyes that go way back, if you know what I mean. When either of them touch their dog, it is so gentle, so full of love. One of the other dog owners, a guy a little rough around the edges, asks what is wrong with Champ. The owners explain that the dog has very bad arthritis, and now his hind legs are giving out, so.... *"You do whatever it takes, right?"* the guy said. *"I got one fifteen years old, he's got real bad arthritis. But it doesn't hurt him. So you know, you do what it takes!"* This guy goes around and pets every dog in the place. Then he sits next to Bill and says, "Can you tell I like animals?"

It was a good clinic. Gabby got some antibiotic eye drops and she's better already. And I felt such love for everybody there. I am nuts about dogs, it's true. And I love other people who feel the same way. But I think the reason I liked being there so much was that there was a group of disparate people all intent on doing a good thing for something they loved. We were bonded, every one of us, and the spirit of hope and willingness and care was so strong. I wanted to raise my hand gaily and say, "Drinks all around!" I wanted to give an impromptu speech about how much I appreciated each and every mutt there—and their owners. Instead, on the way out of the clinic, I locked eyes with Champ's owners, and I was wishing them luck, and more. Strength, maybe. Champ watched us go, and it was as though he were telling me, "Don't worry. I got them." I believed him. Of course I did.

Once Upon a Time in Spring

It was spring in the little town, and all the people were happy. They shed their jackets, they walked their joyful dogs for longer periods of time, they sat outdoors in sidewalk cafes and turned their faces up to the sun. They decided that the earth and all its inhabitants were more benevolent than they had thought. They gazed into the centers of all the vibrant flowers in their gardens and said welcome, welcome! They filled birdbaths so that the warblers could cool off.

The next day, it snowed. No, said most people. All but one said, *Nooooooo*!!!!! And that one said, "Oh, it won't last but a day. Then, it will gradually get warmer again, and you will appreciate spring even more!" And all the rest of the townspeople got together and nailed his doors shut so he couldn't come out and annoy them anymore.

Jealous Soup

Today when I walked Gabby, my hands got really cold, even though I was wearing gloves. So what could I do but come home and make soup? I'm going to give you the recipe, but first I'm going to tell you a little story.

When I was eight, I was over playing dolls with my friend Kathy, who was an only child. When lunch time rolled around, her mother delivered *to her room* two bowls of split-pea soup and two pieces of lavishly buttered toast *on a tray*. With *napkins*. (And probably Kool-Aid to drink in plastic glitter glasses, I wouldn't be a bit surprised.)

I couldn't believe it. I was so jealous that she was treated this way, like a princess. Lunch on a tray! *Plus*: she had way more doll clothes than I. I was very jealous. And when I tasted the soup, oh my, it was unbearably delicious.

I have never been able to make a pea soup that good, and it finally occurred to me that the thing to do was to eat it sitting on my bedroom floor with doll clothes all around me, seething with jealousy. However, I no longer have dolls and doll clothes, and it is too hard to get up when I sit on the floor, so I'm going to eat this soup at the kitchen table and seethe with jealousy in comfort.

One note: this recipe tells you to add some chunky soup to the pureed soup. You can do that, it makes it prettier, I guess. But I like my pea soup all pureed, like sick people soup. Nothing to clunk into your teeth, and you can dip buttered toast into it better when it's smooth, too.

Split-Pea Soup (aka Jealous Soup)

2 T. unsalted butter
Olive oil
1 c. thinly sliced celery
1 c. thinly sliced carrots
1 c. thinly sliced onion
1 clove garlic, minced
1 t. dried marjoram
1 bay leaf
1 t. kosher salt
1/2 t. freshly ground black pepper
1 c. split peas, rinsed and sorted
1 qt. chicken broth
2 c. water
1 c. frozen green peas, thawed
1 c. whipping cream (or half-and-half or milk)

Optional first step: Put on some great '40's music.

1. In a soup pot, melt butter into 2 T. warmed oil over medium heat. Add celery, carrots, onion, garlic, marjoram, bay leaf, salt and pepper. Cook, stirring now and then, until vegetables are fragrant and softened, about ten minutes.

2. Stir in split peas, broth and water. Bring to a boil, reduce to a simmer and cook, partially covered, stirring regularly, until thick, about one hour.

3. Pull out bay leaf. Scoop out one cup soup. Add defrosted peas to pot. Use an immersion blender to swirl soup smooth. Return chunky cup of soup to pot. Stir in cream. Get really jealous of something and eat.

Peace Be with You

The first and perhaps the most important requirement for a successful writing performance—and writing is a performance, like singing an aria or dancing a jig—is to understand the nature of the occasion. -Stephen Greenblatt

I found this quote to be so interesting. And I guess it speaks to what I'm trying to do now in my work, which is to provide a place of respite and hope. To remind myself and others that most people are mostly good.

Last night, Bill told me about yet another shooting. And I felt that familiar ache in my chest, and I said, "I don't even know what to say anymore."

But that's the most dangerous thing, to stop speaking out in times such as these. For every heinous act we see or read about, we need to respond in whatever way we can with all the goodness and humanity and even optimism that we can muster up. Personally. Politically. We need to be as vigilant as we can. We need to hold people responsible for their actions. We need to use our talents, whatever they may be, to try to reshape the narrative we are seeing play out before us into something that respects the earth and its inhabitants.

All of what we are enduring now is so hard to take, even for those of us who are only bystanders. Although, even as I write this, I think, who is just a bystander anymore?

I was moved by the image of two people who were holding each other as they watched the flames burn in California. It reminded me that what we always have as our best resource is each other. Let us work toward resolution of our many problems in some way every day. And let us remember, too, that love and art and music and literature and even food go a long way toward helping us care for ourselves while we try to take care of others. Let's put our own oxygen masks on, and then reach out to others.

I am no longer a practicing Catholic, but I always liked these words in the Mass, and I offer them to you now:

Peace be with you. And with your spirit.

Giving

So I read this poem (that I'll put at the end of this post) on *The Writer's Almanac* this morning. (*The Almanac* is back! You can subscribe for free if you want, and you'll get an offering every day that will probably inspire you and possibly sustain you.)

The gift this particular poem brought me is the idea of giving to others, spontaneously, out of a sense of joyousness—blunted by exhaustion though it may be.

I once was at a store and witnessed a woman complimenting another woman on her earrings. That woman promptly removed her earrings and gave them to the woman who had complimented her. She was met with protest: "Oh, I couldn't, oh no, oh no." But the other woman insisted, and so the woman who admired the earrings went home with them. She got more than earrings, of course. She got a reminder of the kindness and generosity that live in the human soul. She got a little lamp of wonder lit, she and everyone who witnessed this event.

Here's something else, sort of related. When the Exxon Valdez oil spill happened in Alaska, a woman I knew when I was living in Massachusetts said she had put herself on a volunteer list to go and help. She might or might not get called, she said, but if she did get called, she'd go at the last minute. I said, "Boy, that will be expensive, to buy an airline ticket from Massachusetts to Alaska at the last minute." "Yes," she said. "That's why I work."

This is my little gift to you this morning, a reminder that after disaster, or in any kind of bleak times, a deeply spiritual willingness remains and asserts itself. We have in us a beautiful light that shows itself in the darkest times. Here's to us all showing it more, on the smallest of occasions, for the big results it delivers—both to the ones we gift, and to ourselves for making such an offering. How about you gift someone with something today— even if it's just good wishes—for no reason. Because it's not for no reason.

Recuerdo *(Memory)*
by Edna St. Vincent Millay
Public Domain

We were very tired, we were very merry—
We had gone back and forth all night on the ferry.
It was bare and bright, and smelled like a stable—
But we looked into a fire, we leaned across a table,
We lay on a hilltop underneath the moon;
And the whistles kept blowing, and the dawn came
        soon.

We were very tired, we were very merry—
We had gone back and forth all night on the ferry;
And you ate an apple, and I ate a pear,
From a dozen of each we had bought somewhere;
And the sky went wan, and the wind came cold,
And the sun rose dripping, a bucketful of gold.

We were very tired, we were very merry,
We had gone back and forth all night on the ferry.
We hailed, "Good morrow, mother!" to a shawl-covered
    head,
And bought a morning paper, which neither of us read;
And she wept, "God bless you!" for the apples and pears,
And we gave her all our money but our subway fares.

Good Will

When I was in nursing school, they taught us about Maslow's hierarchy of needs, a pyramid that showed that you needed to have one thing before you could advance up to the next level. When I think of our world today, I think of it being like that pyramid. If we don't have a planet on which to live, then none of us can advance to anything else. So I have done my own research, to say nothing of having witnessed more and more frequently the results of increasingly chaotic weather patterns, and I have deduced that climate change is real. For those who are the so-called climate deniers, what harm would it do to act as though it is real? What would we lose? Jobs? Redirect jobs into clean energy jobs.

When people are being shot on campuses and in classrooms, in movie theaters, in churches and synagogues, at concerts, in yoga studios—and more—how can we feel safe? How can we advance up the pyramid if we're dead? So I support mental health programs *and* gun control legislation. For those who do not, I ask again, what would it hurt to enact such legislation?

I don't want to start a big firestorm here. I don't want a lot of nasty comments directed my way or toward anyone else. I welcome civil discussion; I think we can all learn from it.

But if you're going to vote for a president based on what's in your wallet, I hope you'll reconsider and vote based on your conscience and on the goodness that I know is in your heart. I want people to do well, to have enough, to get paid what they are worth. I want my country to love and have pride in itself. I think it's fair to ask the question: what should we be proud of?

I know there are people whose politics are radically different from my own, but I also know that if we met at the eggplant bin at the grocery store, we could have a swell chat about what we were making with the eggplant, and we could both walk away feeling good. As much as a platitude as it sounds like, let us start there, in recognizing that we really do have things in common that link us all together. Envision a virtual circle of good intention and good will, all of us there, where one talks, and all the rest listen. Round and round the circle. I believe we have it in us to love one another. To find ways to work together toward a greater good that serves us all. I believe peace is possible. I really do. I also believe that time is running out. And so I hope that whatever the election results are, we can get out the big Band-Aids and the big binoculars, to take care of the big hurts and to look forward to a better future. It truly is in our hands.

Moving Day

Yesterday, I was taking Gabby for a walk when I passed by a neighbor's house. She was sitting out on her front porch steps, wearing a simple cotton dress, sneakers and white socks, and a sweatshirt jacket. It was Moving Day, and all her things had been loaded up in a van, and the van had just taken off. We talked a bit about where she was going, which was to a condo nearby ("Really small," she said, "but big enough for me.") She's been through a very difficult and drawn-out situation after a divorce, and I was glad to see that she had finally been able to sell her house, and that now, hopefully, her life would calm down and even out. But I was sorry to see her go. She was my neighbor. She had a distinctive, loud laugh. She had a good dog, a beautiful Husky that I always liked to see and pet. I wanted to tell her that, although we didn't hang out a lot, I kind of relied on her being there. In keeping her place, she held me in mine. My friend Mary, who is from Poland, once said, "In my country, we say people like old trees. Not like to move." As an Army brat, I moved a lot, and although there was always something exciting about going to a new place, it was hard to leave the old place, too. It was always as though the place you left watched you go, it was as though the windows of the place you were leaving were its eyes, turned toward you in a mild kind of sorrow as you drove away.

After I came home from walking Gabby, my neighbor was gone, and I stood in front of her house for a while, and I looked the windows, those house eyes, which offered nothing but blank acceptance. It's an old house, and I wondered about all the people who had lived there before. And now it will be someone new moving in, and I'll bake them some chocolate chip cookies as a welcome to the neighborhood. But I'll still see the ghost of my old neighbor and her dog, waving from across the street, or stopping to talk, or doubled over, laughing, out on the sidewalk in front of my house, the sound traveling up through my office window.

"People not like to move."

I think that's true for many of us. Also, people not like to watch people move.

The Little Things

Today I wrote to a friend having some health problems that we have arrived at a funny time of life. Not *so* near the end, but getting there—it's as though our brains keep receiving pop-up ads featuring intimations on mortality. It seems to me that the thing to do now is to figure out how best to move forward, in joy and clarity, toward what enriches our souls most. One of the good parts of getting older is that this idea, which probably should be worked on for the whole of our lifetimes, finally becomes an imperative. For me, what brings joy has always been the little things. Such as: yesterday, I stood in the kitchen at the open back door with a cup of caramel flavored coffee, and looked out into the yard. I saw a stand of yellow daffodils, a bunny, a robin, and uneven tufts of green grass that looked like a bad but charming haircut. Check.

Yesterday, while I was in the car waiting at a red light, I saw a man out walking what looked like a Coonhound. He was a young dog, very exuberant, and having a hard time settling down on the leash. The man told him to sit, and the dog looked up at him, practically trembling with his desire to please. He sat. And so he got a treat. And his tail wagged and wagged as they stepped off the curb and I thought, check, there's another one.

In world that feels full of so many difficult problems, it's good to know that some things are so easy.

A Little on Aging

There is cleaning out drawers and closets, and then there is cleaning things off your computer. Digging around today, I found the beginning of an essay I wanted to write about aging. It's just the beginning, but it occurs to me now that it's all I want or need to say about that subject: Wendell Barry's poem "*VII*" has in it these lines: "I don't think of myself as an old man. I think of myself as a young man with unforeseen difficulties."

That's a variation of something I heard a lot when I was a nurse and took care of the elderly: "Inside, I'm still a girl." It's one thing to be a pink-cheeked 24-year-old hearing words like this, and another altogether to be a 70-year-old woman hearing them. At this age, one doesn't just hear them; one feels them.

Sometimes I look into the mirror trying to get a sense of what will happen to me, aging wise; and what I see reflected back is every one of us. We might as well be mice dangling by our tails, held between the Great Experimenter's fingers. Because I understand that anything can happen to anyone, at any age—isn't the evidence everywhere? Still, as we age, the possibility of something dire happening becomes more likely. Not long ago, I listed how many of my peers/ friends I've lost: ten.

But guess what? Most days, this makes for a feeling not of sadness or helplessness or rage but of great tenderness and resolve. What is there to do but to live one's best life, and go out and find someone to be kind to? Or to endeavor to be like

one of my friends who is at the moment having a
whole world of problems, but who called me last
night only to say how full of joy she was that the
night was clear and the stars brilliant?

Self-Promotion

When I was a sophomore in high school, I ran for
vice president of the sophomore class. My Dad
printed out some flyers for me to hand out, and I
did hand out some, maybe two. I was too embarrassed to hand out more. When voting day came, I
did not vote for myself, because I thought it would
be rude. I did nothing to promote myself because it
was just too excruciating. Guess what? I became
vice president of the sophomore class anyway,
because I ran unopposed. I then went on to do not
much, which I believe is the job description for
many vice presidents but hey! I got to use the word
"ex officio" in my acceptance speech on the advice
of a teacher who thought it would sound swell.

This is a long way of saying that I, like many
shy authors, have a hard time promoting myself
when a new book comes out. I do all my homework
assignments for my publisher, I post things on
Facebook, but the only thing I really like doing is
going out on tour and being face to face with
people who actually read my books. On those
occasions, I feel as though it's a different kind of
Christmas and I'm unwrapping friends.

So before all the promoting begins in earnest, I
just want to say a quieter thank you to all of you who
have shown such support already, including telling
me that you'll be at this signing or that. I'll be looking
for you, you betcha.

Rainy Day Soup

So gray and rainy outside, it feels like the day is pouting. Gabby is sitting at the kitchen door and looking out, trying to will away the bad weather away. So far: weather 1, Gabby, 0.

I am ignoring a hamper full of dirty laundry and organizing recipes I've been wanting to try, but now I have to leave to go the thrift store. I feel certain something there is waiting for me. It might be a bowl! I have a great love for bowls with personality. I can never have enough of them, even though I have too many of them.

I made this soup today while I listened to a John Legend CD:

Chicken Avocado Lime Soup
Servings: 6 servings
Prep Time 15 minutes. Cook Time 20 minutes.

1 1/2 lbs boneless skinless chicken breasts*
1 T. olive oil
1 c. chopped green onions
2 jalapeños, seeded and minced (leave seeds if you want soup spicy, omit if you don't like heat)
2 cloves garlic, minced
4 (14.5 oz) cans low-sodium chicken broth
2 Roma tomatoes, seeded and diced
1/2 t. ground cumin
Salt and freshly ground black pepper
1/3 c. chopped cilantro
3 T. fresh lime juice
3 medium avocados, peeled, cored and diced

Tortilla chips, Monterey Jack cheese, sour cream for serving (optional)

*If breasts are thick, cut in half through the length of the breasts. They will cook faster and more evenly.

1. In a large pot heat 1 T. olive oil over medium heat. Once hot, add green onions and jalapenos and sauté until tender, about two minutes, adding garlic during last 30 seconds of sautéing.

2. Add chicken broth, tomatoes, cumin, season with salt and pepper to taste and add chicken breasts. Bring mixture to a boil over medium-high heat.

3. Then reduce heat to medium, cover with lid and allow to cook, stirring occasionally, until chicken has cooked through 10-15 minutes (cook time will vary based on thickness of chicken breasts).

4. Reduce burner to warm heat, remove chicken from pan and let rest on a cutting board five minutes, then shred chicken and return to soup. Stir in cilantro and lime juice.

5. Add avocados to soup just before serving (if you don't plan on serving the soup right away, I would recommend adding the avocados to each bowl individually, about 1/2 an avocado per serving). Serve with tortilla chips, cheese and sour cream if desired.

Recipe from www.cookingclassy.com

P.S. This just in. I changed my mind. I don't need to buy *anything*. I need to go and lie under my magic blanket and read. When the rain comes down harder, it will be lovely.

Gabby: Says you.

Life. Love. Music. Art.

I just came back from seeing *A Star is Born*. I went
to see it at ten in the morning because I just
couldn't wait. There I sat in the dark when I
suppose I should have been working, my umbrella
as my seatmate, my eyes and ears glued to the
screen.

First of all, a star *is* born—Lady Gaga was
terrific.

Also: That movie reached in and grabbed my
heart out of my chest, threw it against the wall a
couple of times, stomped on it, sliced it up, and
then put it back in my chest, gently.

It's a love story, but it's as much about love of
music as of people. I was transported back to my
twenties when I sang in a band. I knew a lot of
musicians then, and whenever I listened to music
with them, I saw every note, every nuance, play out
across their faces. I learned so much about music
from watching them. And from my roommate in
1969, Lois, who introduced me to Odetta and the
super smooth Lou Rawls: *When I was 21, it was a
very good year....* Oh, and Buffy St. Marie. Leonard
Cohen. Probably Miles Davis, too. Morgana King:
When it all comes true, just the way you planned....

I miss a lot of things about being younger,
primary among them being the ability to get down
onto and up off the floor in one effortless
movement. But perhaps most of all I miss the way
my friends and I used to share music. The new
Beatles album would come out, and there we'd be,
huddled around the stereo, listening; nothing

mattered more. I remember exactly where I was and how I felt the first time I heard Janis Joplin. (*Summertime*, she growled, and my eyes popped wide open.) I lay on my living room floor listening to Leonard Bernstein's *Kaddish* with my friend Phyllis, and we clenched our fists over our hearts and squeezed our eyes shut and said the words along with the narrator: "Tin god! Your covenant is tin, it crumples in my hand!"

It's hard to hold onto everything in life that once was precious to us. It's not because it's not precious any longer, it's just that somehow things narrow, and we can't fit everything in that we might like to. But I'm so grateful for a movie or a play or a book or a poem or a painting that lifts me up and puts me back down in a familiar, loved place, if only for a brief time. Even if it hurts so bad, it makes you tremble. Which is what I was doing when I came out of that movie. I crossed the street to Poke Burrito and when I picked up the slip of paper to write down my order, my hands were shaking. And when I spoke, I said, "May I have brown rice with that?" but what I was really saying was, "Oh, my God. Life. Love. Music. Art. Aren't we lucky?

A Club For Gabby

Misery loves company, they say. It seems to be true. After feeling bad about Gabby needing a trip to the vet and having to wear the cone of shame, I was sent a photo of someone else's dog wearing a cone. Immediately, my spirits lifted. A club for Gabby! I tried to show the photo to Gabby but she is too smart to waste her time looking at screens. She wants her reality straight up real, no virtual about it, thank you very much.

There's a quote I really love by the poet W.B. Yeats: "Being Irish, he had an abiding sense of tragedy which sustained him through temporary periods of joy." This resonates for me because I am part Irish and I always go to *that* place. A beleaguered elementary school teacher of mine who otherwise seemed to like me very much once wrote on my report card: Elizabeth needs to learn to overcome these moody spells.

But I felt better after I saw the photo, and I got my priorities straightened out. Gabby just had a hot spot, after all. Nothing more.

But then I went to sleep. And in sleep, sometimes the imps come out with their long gray hair and their long yellow fingernails and they squat on top of my head and do a little creative—which is to say malevolent—brain rearranging. And so my brain began to talk to my subconscious, saying, "You think that's a hot spot, huh? Is that what you think? Well, let me ask you something. Do you remember the trouble you had with Homer's paw, which you thought at first was nothing?

Remember what happened with Homer, who ended up having a malignant melanoma?" I woke up full of fear and sadness and overwhelming love for Gabby who truly is my best friend. I'm afraid I annoyed her a bit with over-petting. She had to kind of walk away and suggest over shoulder that maybe I should feed her a cookie, wouldn't that make us both feel better?

I had to remind myself that Gabby is not Homer. And even if she were, she would be the dog that was loved to the nth degree, and who loved his roommates (Bill and me) back in the same way.

The highest thing we ask for in life is what is manifested between dogs and the people who really, really love them. That's what I think, anyway.

And now I think I'll go and buy an eight-foot ladder at the hardware store. Just call me John Wayne. Or Jane Wayne. In full disclosure, the real reason I'm going is not just to buy the ladder. The hardware store is very close to Peterson's ice cream, home of the best turtle sundae. Let's see how the old will power does today. I think I can guess.

Going Home

A trip to the Minnesota State Fair this year let me know I'm not quite nine years old anymore. Or 49, for that matter. I ate far less than I usually do. I walked less, saw fewer things. Oh, I saw the chickens all right, you have to see the chickens, because they are so fun and expressive and some seem to be wearing go-to-church hats that split the difference between gorgeous and hilarious. I saw the magnificent Clydesdales, and wondered, as I always do, if they enjoyed all the pomp and ceremony as much as their owners/drivers seem to. Those horses are the living definition of "prance with dignity." I went to the art building and admired everything and got pretty hopeful about all that creativity can do for us. I saw all the fabulous scarecrows in the agricultural building, and the seed art and the flower arrangements. I went to the food building, naturally, and I saw the butter heads being sculpted. I watched a guy hawk some pans that were outrageously expensive and I kept wanting to raise my hand and say, "Excuse me, but you can get All-Clad with the copper insert for less than that! Plus you are doing way too much fear-mongering and guilt tripping." (I'll spare you the details of the guy's pitch.) I did not go on the Old Mill ride, which I regret, because it's a nice tradition and it would have been cool on a hot day to go in the darkness that the ride provides. Oh, that ride used to be so racy; you could *kiss* on it, and no one would see you!

When Bill and I drove home the next day, we took the beautiful Great River Road on the Wisconsin side. We made a stop soon into it, at the Stockholm Pie and General store, for obvious reasons. I bought cheese and sausage and flour sack dishtowels with farm animals on them. And oh my goodness, the pie there was so good, both the sweet and the savory varieties. *And* they had pie cookies, little baby pies that you could gobble in two bites. I had a pie cookie and then bought ten more to take home. Also, I bought two little pies perfect for serving four (or just me)—bumbleberry and cherry. Adorable pies. I want to name something Bumbleberry. Maybe a mayor in a children's book.

As we drove on, the air was too still, and the sky, although not green, was not a common color. It turned out that we drove right into flood and tornado country. Roads were closed, and we ended up backtracking quite a bit. In one town, where we saw a barn in a low area with water half way up its sides, we also saw mudslides and trees down. We got an emergency warning on the cell phone for more storms coming. We weren't quite sure what direction we should go in. There was a utility truck parked near where we had pulled over to let Gabby out and plan our route. Bill went over to talk to the guy to see if he had any advice. They talked for a long time while I sat nervously picking at my fingernails, and when Bill got back in the car, he knew which way to go, and it was not something we could have figured out on our own. The guy made a special call for us, in the midst of all the other things he was doing. Bill thanked him, but it was only when we were about fifty miles away that something occurred to me: "We should have given him a pie!" I said. And Bill said yeah, we should have. At least. But there was no turning back. As it was, it took us fifteen hours to get back to Chicago.

I keep thinking of that man. I am still so grateful to him for taking the time to offer help to strangers at a time when he was so taxed himself. I think, though, that the man *wanted* to help, because in doing so, he helped himself as much as he did us. I guess that's the lesson we relearn every time we exercise kindness: it goes both ways, it always goes both ways. I only wish I'd given that guy a pie. I wish I'd given him all of the pies except for one raspberry cookie pie, which I would have shared with Bill when we arrived safely home.

Everybody says the best words are "I love you." For me, though, it's "safely home." I guess it's the same thing.

Random Acts of Kindness

I see that in a very nice review of *Night of Miracles* someone has noted that I have moved firmly into the realm of "cozy." I guess that's right. I guess I'm back to my role of nurse, wanting to comfort people so that I myself might be comforted. Thank you to every single one of you who read me, for staying with me on this long and interesting journey we've been on for the last two years. I can hardly wait until we can all breathe again. Maybe then I'll write a horror book. But probably not. Probably I'll focus on the joy of the little things for the rest of my natural life. Here's to daisies in a kitchen glass, centered on the table, and to the feel of your dog's head under your hand in the morning before you've even opened your eyes. To deserted churches where you can sit and feel a kind of peace in the air like humidity. To the smell of sugar and butter in the air at bakeries and to their display cases that send you into paroxysms of indecision. To the honest and charmingly tactless inquires of young children. To the cocked heads of the robins. To violets growing at the base of a tree. To random acts of kindness, which we need now more than ever, that common miracle of one little good thing from you, becoming so big for someone else.

So Long, KitchenAid Mixer

In 1985, when I began to write articles for magazines, I used one of my first checks to buy a KitchenAid Mixer, which I had longed for forever. Today, it died. Well, it still works, but it only will go on one speed, which is high. I have cake batter splattered all over my kitchen counter, but I don't mind. Thank you for your many years of service is what I say. Thanks for cakes and cookies and banana bread and mashed potatoes and whew, I don't know what all.

I'm giving my mixer a funeral in ten minutes. In lieu of sending flowers, please use your mixer to make a cake today. And when it has finished mixing, pat it and say, "Thanks a lot, pal. I'm glad you're here."

A Cure for Sadness

There are days that happen to all of us when we just feel...off. The feeling is akin to sadness, but it's a kind of irritating sadness, a gnat-like thing that you just can't bat away. I had such a day today, and I had to drag out my imaginary bureau of sorrows to see what might be up. Was it health worries about me or my loved ones? No. Was it some re-awakened memory of that wretched boy who broke my heart all those years ago? No. Was it missing people who have gone from the earth? Nope. I cruised around FB, as many people do when they're sad, looking for some company, for some relief. And I came across a video of a white man on a train screaming at another man for being Chinese. Pointing his finger and him and saying, "I hate you Chinese!" And I thought, Oh. That's it. That's what's bothering me. It's the low-flame anxiety and despair that has been with me for a long time now, a despair that comes from watching the rising levels of intolerance and incivility all around me. At least other passengers on the train gathered around the Chinese man to protect him.

What does one do about this, other than try to monitor one's own behavior and work in whatever way possible toward truth and justice as one sees it? Eat, of course.

I decided to made a yellow cake and though I almost always bake from scratch, this time I used a mix and it was so good I ate way too much and then I lay upon my sofa full not only of carbohydrates but of self-loathing.

Not much help.

So I leashed up Gabby and went out for a walk and my heart immediately jerked and pulled forward like it was tethered to a big helium balloon. Because:

—I saw fireflies rise up in their slow and magical way (don't they look somehow *specifically* weighted?) from a garden where wild strawberries and wild ginger were growing.

—I saw a cloud that looked exactly like the state of Maine which, before my eyes, broke apart to become something that now looked like the state of Michigan next to a rearing stallion. I swear this is true.

—On the sidewalk that goes through a park by a school, I was passed by a young couple on their bikes, maybe sixteen years old. Very beautiful children. When they rode past a little fountain in the park that is a playful fountain—spurting up here one moment, there the next—I heard her cry out in her sweet, high voice, "Oh!" And he, in his adolescent boy's lower voice, said, "Oh. Wow." I came upon them again at the swing set. Their bikes lay companionably side by side in the dirt and the boy and girl were on the bucket swings, moving back and forth and talking, but not looking at each other. Very shy and beautiful children. Then they rose up together and grabbed their bikes and she said, "Oh, hey! You know what?" and then he did look at her. I wanted to hang around and hear what she had to say, but you know. Very shy and beautiful children who were entitled to their privacy.

—I passed sunflowers way taller than I and some corn—*corn!* big stalks of corn like in the movie Oklahoma!—that the school children had planted and I hoped that they had gotten a chance to come back and see what they had wrought.

—The light changed to a kind of sepia tone, and all of a sudden things looked like a past that I was moving through in the present.

—I veered off from the sidewalk to walk home through the park-like median strip that runs for only a few blocks, and what a good decision that was. There were a lot of rabbits who were doing their *I'm-going-to-hold-very-still-and-that-way-you won't-see-me* trick until they panicked and did their *I'm-going to-hop-away-and-my-white-cottontail-bouncing-up-and down-will-make-you-laugh-out-loud* trick.

—Darkness came and all the stars' alarm clocks went off and they started showing up for work. We don't see a lot of stars here and I think if we all saw more stars we would all be better off.

Anyway, all the irritating sadness is gone now. I saw these things, I talked to you all, and now I'm going to put on my most comfortable (i.e. soft and ragged) pajamas and read.

I do realize my own great luck. Thank you for your time.

Piece of Cake

Oh, man. Trader Joe's yellow cake mix is really good! (How could it not be when it calls for a whole stick of butter?) I just had some with peaches and vanilla ice cream on top. Now I need to go for a little walk to burn the calories off. Fifty miles or so ought to do it.

Update: I ate another piece. I thought it would help if I ate it outside because my body *might* think I was exercising. Nope. Now I feel like a well-fed tick and my bra is so tight I can't breathe.

Friending

I would like to tell all the people who have asked to be friends on this page, and haven't gotten an answer, that it's me, not you. Really. I have had some bad experiences friending (is that the term? *Should* that be a term?) people I don't know and now I look at the photos of people asking to be friends and I wring my hands and think.....I don't know, I don't know.

"Only friend people you know!" my friends tell me. But I don't know a *lot* of you who post here and I *do* feel like you're my friends.

I don't know how to work most of the tech-related things I do. On the computer, I (sort of) learned what I have to in order to post here and to write my books and answer email. (It wasn't that long ago that I had to ask what a browser was. I still think it's mostly a good name for a dog. Plus why do they use the word "cookies" for computers, which *really* mixes me up? When I hear "cookies," I have only one response: "Where?" And to me, "URL" sounds like a digestive ailment. Or a call you make in the wild to attract moose.)

I live in fear that my "keyless" entry to my car will stop working. I'm baffled by my slow cooker, but I do manage to figure that out each time I use it, because, you know, it's food. I like the old bathroom scales with the needle indicator rather than the...what? LED display? I mean, to the extent that I like scales.

I'm confused about how to download music so I only listen to the radio and CDs and vinyl, only now my stereo is ill and won't play vinyl. I realize I could learn some things, but I'd rather learn how to make delicious vegan dishes and how to create a garden that bees and butterflies will come to and how to improve my crummy but full-of-love quilts. I want to read and sit on the porch and take walks and go to movies and plays and concerts and to watch my super duper grandchildren be themselves. And a girl only has so much time. So please know that I am not rejecting you if I don't answer your request to be friends on this page. I'm just surrendering to my incompetence and hoping that you'll still drop by to visit here. As Fred Rogers said, won't you (still) be my neighbor?

I am reading *There There* by Tommy Orange. Brilliant.

I am eating Ina Garten's goat cheese and roasted red pepper sandwich on a ciabatta roll.

I loved the Mr. Rogers movie; it made me weep.

I love, too, the fireflies who are out in full force every evening now. If you feel sad about something, watch those guys. You will feel as if your soul stepped right on the elevator to Feeling Better Land.

Also, you could watch a little kid wipe ice cream off his fingers and onto his t-shirt. Different prescription; same cure.

Ditto dogs, but hey, this is getting long. See you later.

The News

A writer asked on FB today if any other writers are having trouble working, given the news we are subjected to each day. My answer is, yes and no. My heart is heavy almost every day, and sometimes it seems almost silly to keep on writing, especially fiction. But one of the things I do to help myself is to write things that remind me of the goodness in life. And so today I read the paper on the front porch and sat very quietly for a while. I said, also very quietly, "Yikes." Then I filled the saucer I keep on a table on the porch with seed for Mr. and Mrs. Cardinal. I don't know how they get away with being the only birds that get that mix but I guess they flaunt their great beauty, as great beauties sometimes do. They probably make the robins and sparrows feel they can't partake. I offer things to the non-cardinal birds in the back yard and also I have a little cage of heatproof suet that I hang in a bush right outside the window where we watch TV. Every time a bird comes to eat there, it feels like my heart glows like E.T.'s.

I just put the ingredients in the slow cooker to make jerk chicken and pineapple sliders for dinner.

Now I'm going to Mason, the fictional town in my last two books, and in the one I'm working on as well. It's a very small town. Nobody much locks their doors. The occasional smallmindedness aside, people are kind to one another. They see each other. Maybe that's how kindness always starts.

Mexican Chicken

Guess what I'm having for dinner? This is such a great summer recipe, and so easy, and I can't find it on line, so I'm going to type out just the directions with the ingredients capitalized. Okay?

Baked Mexican Chicken Breasts

Turn on some music, Hank Williams might be nice. Put on your apron. Food turns out better if you wear an apron because it thinks you're a pro. Turn oven on to 375. Put 4 T. BUTTER in a shallow baking pan big enough to hold six CHICKEN BREASTS and put it in the oven for the butter to melt. Meanwhile, in a shallow bowl, mix 2 EGGS with 3 T. GREEN CHILE SALSA (or any salsa) and 1/4 t. SALT. In another shallow bowl, mix 1 cup fine BREAD CRUMBS, 1 t. each of CHILI POWDER and GROUND CUMIN, 3/4 t. GARLIC SALT, 1/4 t. OREGANO. Dip chicken breasts in wet mix, then dry, then repeat (it's fine if you just do it once). Bake, uncovered, for about 35 minutes or until meat in thickest section of breast is done. Your kitchen will smell swell. Your dog will wander in and say, "What's cooking? It smells so good!" Your cat will roll her eyes.

To serve, arrange chicken breasts on a bed of 4-6 cups of LETTUCE (the recipe says iceberg lettuce, but I like a mix of butter and spring mix). Garnish with 1-2 LIMES cut into quarters, 12-18 CHERRY TOMATOES, 1 AVOCADO sliced, 4 thinly sliced GREEN ONIONS, and about 1 cup SOUR

CREAM. Pass around extra sour cream and salsa at the table.

Serve with corn muffins that you make yourself. Or you can cheat and use Trader Joe's corn muffin mix, it's great.

This is so good. Honestly. I'm going to go and eat it now. I've made it six million times and I *still* get excited when I make it.

The Sticky Middle

A summer night, and Bill and I are taking Gabby for a walk, and talking about the restaurant incident with Sarah Huckabee Sanders. I don't like that it happened, but at the same time I understand that when people don't feel heard, when they feel threatened, they act out. We have a long conversation that comes back to a familiar tenet: violence begets violence. I am so afraid of what this country is becoming. I fear for all of us, especially for my six-week-old grandson, whose soft spots haven't even closed yet. We got quiet for a while, Bill and I, and I watched the fireflies appearing and disappearing in their magical way and I saw how the white flowers in people's gardens seemed to glow and I saw a thin black cloud place itself over the full moon. I felt a kind of sadness mixed with a longing, and I felt the usual sense of confusion and despair over what to do. "I wish I could invite Sarah over," I said suddenly. "I wish we could get together and make a vow to not talk politics at all, but instead, oh, I don't know, I could say, "Those pearls you often wear. Do they carry any special meaning for you?" I could ask what books she likes, what movies, what recipes, what TV shows, what kind of weather. I could ask about her children." But in this fantasy, everything became very pointed, somehow. If I asked about her children, would I not also be asking about the migrant children? "Let me ask you something," I said to Bill. "And I think I know what you're going to answer. But do you think she believes what she says to the press in those briefings?" Bill sighed. "It's all just a game," he said.

Gabby Talks

Me: Gabby! Gabby! Did you see? The robins are building a nest over the garage light again! Same place as they did a couple of years ago! Remember how we loved watching them? Want to help build the nest?

Gabby: Um. I think they do that themselves.

Me: Yes, but we can help with raw materials. I have dryer lint. You have hair. Come here, let me brush you a little.

Gabby: You have hair, too.

Me: I know, but it's not as good for nests as yours.

Gabby: [Stands there]

Me: Come here! Let me brush you!

Gabby: [Walks over. Very slowly. Very, very slowly. Because for some reason she hates being brushed.]

Me: [Brushing] Good girl! Ohhhhh, look at all this good stuff on your tail! You've got such a great, fluffy tail!

Gabby: [Stares resolutely forward. After being brushed, shakes as though there's water all over her, then goes and lies down far away from me.]

Me: This is great. I'll just go and put it outside. [I put the hair and the dryer lint on the ground. Then I decide to put it closer to the nest, and I drape it over the bottom of the trellis beneath the light. Then I move it up to the top of the trellis. Then the birds stop coming.] Oh, Gabby. The robins stopped building their nest.

Gabby: I'm not saying anything. Although if I did say something, I'd say you should *not* have interfered. They know what they're doing. They don't need your help! And they probably like to pick their own materials. You're like a food worker standing behind the counter where people say or point to what they want and you're just merrily piling *your* choices on their plates! "How about some of these wonderful mashed potatoes?" THWACK! "Oh, these green beans are great, real buttery!" THWACK!

Me: You're right. You're right. Plus the birds probably smell me, and I think birds hate the smell of humans. Oh, now I've ruined everything! I will never learn not to be controlling. Never, never, never!

Gabby: Oy. You were a dramatic child and now you are a dramatic adult.

Me: I know. [Sniffs]

Gabby: Take me for a walk, why don't you? Get your mind off it.

A few hours later:

Me: Gabby! They came back! They're building the nest again! Look how they spread their feathers and settle in there to shape the nest to fit them!

Gabby: Yes, I see. Now I'm going to tell you to look at something else.

Me: What?

Gabby: The back door. See the back door?

Me: Duh. I'm standing in front of it.

Gabby: Do not go past it. Leave those birds alone.

Me: What about when I have to go into the garage?

Gabby: Then go into the garage. Do not stop to talk to the birds or look at the nest close up or put hair or lint or anything else next to them. Deal?

Me: [Sighs] Deal.

Gabby: Shake hands on it?
         [We shake.]

Gabby: Good girl.

Heart and Humanity

Today I came down into the kitchen and saw the front page of the New York Times. The image looked like a concentration camp, and my already broken heart broke some more.

When there are terrible differences between people, I always hope that reason and dialogue will help. No one is *all* bad. No one is all good, either. We have differing points of view on all kinds of things: art, music, literature. But we are all human beings gifted with certain commonalities, among them hearts. Whatever you believe about why people try to come to this country, you cannot believe that babies and toddlers must pay the price.

"What should we do?" I ask Bill, all but wringing my hands. Call your congressperson, yes, but many times when you try, you can't get through. I thought about chartering a bus to go to Texas with others to protest: hold up a sign, chant, something. What I really wanted to do is bring a rocking chair and rock any child who wants such comfort. But, you know, no touching. I talked about having Jeffersonian dinners at my house again, where people with different points of view could try to talk things out. Bill talked about dragging a certain someone out of the White House by his little ear.

I am sorry to say that I have come to think that dialogue and compromise won't work. Getting rid of the gangs and violence that make for so many leaving their homes? (And by the way, does anyone really believe that people leave their homes without pain and sorrow and fear? That people blithely say, "I think I'll just go to the United States. That will put me right on Easy Street.")

So yes, getting rid of gangs and violence will help, but how? And when? In the meantime, there is a kind of Sophie's choice for desperate people who want to protect their children and themselves, and are seeking asylum. I don't believe that most of the people who want to come here are "rapists and murderers." I resent the language.

I made a vow a long time ago to make my FB page a place of refuge from the news. We are all so dug in to our respective positions, it is all choirs preaching to choirs. But now it is an emergency of the most heartrending nature. Even if you are pro-wall and pro-Trump, if you believe this warehousing of children is wrong, please speak up in whatever way you can. Honor humanity and heart and responsibility. That's what will "make American great again."

The Movies

I decided to go to see the movie *Book Club*. I figured it would be not very good, but I'll see anything with Diane Keaton in it. I thought about asking someone to go with me, but I wanted to go alone. For a while, I thought-punished myself about that, thinking, what's the matter with you? Why are you so anti-social? But I don't feel that I am, really. I'll chat up strangers with ease, just like my Irish grandfather always did. And I have a lot of friends. Then I remembered the wisdom of something I read recently that talked about the difference between solitude and loneliness: Loneliness is looking inward at the self, solitude is looking outward at the world. I wanted to look outward, by myself. So I took myself out to dinner at Five Guys and I watched the other patrons. One was a woman who kept smacking her teenage son on the arm, on the shoulder, and I was about to interfere, but didn't. And I'm glad I didn't because in a few minutes they were smiling at each other. There was a single man who came in and if ever a human looked like he was licking his chops, it was that guy; he was practically drooling as he placed his order, and who could blame him?

I went to the movie and it didn't start and didn't start and didn't start. The attendees were subjected to music and a graphic for Chevrolet for almost fifteen minutes. Finally I got up and went to the manager's office and told him.

"Oh, okay," he said. "I'll fix it."

So I went back into the theatre and said in a loud voice, "If anyone else was wondering why we've been listening to music for fifteen minutes, please know I just spoke to the manager and we'll be seeing the movie shortly."

"Thank you!" said one man.

"You're welcome!" said I, feeling a little, little bit like Reelwoman, hero of the cinema. Then the movie started and immediately quit. And we all started laughing. And then the movie played. It wasn't a great movie, but there were moments. Seeing that Diane Keaton apparently hasn't had a face lift and lets herself be seen as she is, that was good. A little speech about how even though you know you might get hurt in love, it's always worth trying it, that was good. Another woman who came alone bought herself a popcorn the size of a silo and plunked herself down in her seat with what looked like great content; seeing her do that was good. And on my bike ride home, thinking that love really IS always worth it, that was good. It was just getting dark, and I don't have a light on my bike, so I took less traveled roads and looked at all the lit windows in the houses I passed. I don't know why those lit windows always get me, but they do.

Baby Land

I have been blissfully emerged in baby land, helping to take care of my daughter and the beautiful Nathaniel. It's been 37 years since I last had my own newborn, and it's amazing how the memories come back when you hold that tiny, nearly weightless, silky-headed bundle in your arms. I recalled the rhythm of rocking I did then, the crib and the nursery lamp with a clown holding balloons that lit up for a nightlight. I remembered the changing table with cloth diapers stacked up, the pins for them stuck in a bar of soap to help them slide in, the way you always put your hand beneath so if anyone got stuck, it was you. If that's not a metaphor for parenthood, I don't know what is. I remembered the way I put my baby on my shoulder to rock her to sleep and patted her back with four fingers, then with two fingers, then with no fingers, then lay her down for sleep but stood watching for a long time before I went to take my own rest.

Babies remind you to turn up your love and turn down your bitterness. They reawaken you to the possibilities of enchantment and the worth of innocence. They make you so excited to show someone else the inside of a blossom, the clouds, dogs, a red ball, stars in the sky. I don't know of any other thing that so instantly widens your willingness to look on the good side. How lucky we are, we grandparents, who stand close by to witness the emergence of a new citizen and the turning of two young people into parents, into besotted individuals that you can plainly see are committed for life. Jenny said I could share a photo, so here you go.

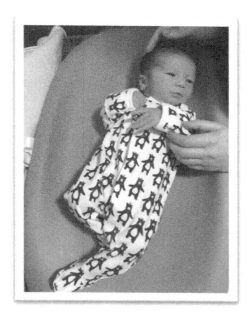

Orchid Miracle

About six or eight months ago, I was given two orchid plants, one yellow, one white. They bloomed for a few months and then that was that. But guess what? They are *both* blooming again. I feel like King Kong, even though I did nothing.

I keep peering at them every day, way close up, with glasses, without glasses. I feel like, *this can't be true*! But it is!

This is a day when I'm just dying for a puppy again. But I'm not going on any puppy sites. Except for now, and then I'm just going to look. Just looking. Unless.

Ghosts

This morning, I made French toast in my grand-father's cast iron pan. After he died, the pan became my mother's, and after my mother died, it became mine. My grandfather, who made the best gravy in the world, used that pan a lot to cook in, a dishtowel tucked into the waistline of his pants. Behind him, the parakeet that he and my grand-mother kept on a TV tray covered with a dish towel chattered and scolded.

My mom used to say that my grandfather made the absolute best Denver sandwiches. Every year, on the day when she and her family went to the Minnesota State Fair, they had those sand-wiches for lunch on a blanket they spread out near Machinery Hill. They couldn't afford the food that was sold at the Fair, but they were better served by those sandwiches and a thermos of coffee.

My mom used the cast iron pan to make goulash and all kinds of other things. Every time I use it, I think of both my grandfather and my mother. I think of how kind my grandfather was, how funny, how his adoration of kids and dogs shone out of his eyes. I think of my mother wearing an apron and making dinner and suffering the whining of always-hungry me. I used to bug her about when dinner would be ready, saying, with my usual dramatic flair, "I'm *starving*."

Once when she was peeling potatoes, she said, "Do you want a raw potato?"

"Yes!" said I, and took it in the living room and lay on my stomach and finished watching Popeye, who made eating spinach look good, though I wasn't too sure about his method of eating it by inhaling it thorough a pipe.

I am continually working on things in my life, including compassion. Including not being so quick to judge or criticize (so far my grade point average on the latter two is F-.) I also want to learn not to be attached to things.

But that pan. I am attached to that pan and I hope I always will be. You slam it down on the burner, light the flame beneath it, and there they all are again. My grandfather. My mom. The parakeet. The milling crowds at the Minnesota State Fair.

Some ghosts break your heart. But others fill it up.

Spring Walking

Now the flowers are strutting their stuff and the air is blessedly mild and the conversations you over-hear on walks seem to float in the air right up to you. Today I heard a young mother who was walking behind me and pushing a stroller with a toddler and a baby say, "Remember when you made that chalk drawing on the sidewalk and it stayed for so long? It stayed for so long! I think it was red."

She was pushing her babies and talking on her cell, but a little part of her was a girl again, maybe standing watching her friend do that drawing on the sidewalk. And maybe after that they both lay on the sidewalk and the heat pushed through their thin shirts so that they felt a very pleasant nothingness, a suspension of sorts like it seems we are meant to achieve in yoga class. And maybe after that they went in for a lunch that someone had prepared for them and then went out again. Or maybe not.

For part of my youth, when I lived on an army base in Texas, we kids were only in our houses to eat, sleep and do homework. And to watch Saturday cartoons. Or to get money so we could buy donuts from the donut lady, who drove around in a station wagon with these amazingly long pull-out drawers full of donuts. Her whole car smelled like it, too, had been glazed. Our parents never knew where any of us were. But they trusted us to come back to eat, sleep, do homework, beg for money and watch cartoons. The music of our summers was a banging screen door, and the movie of our summers was the fading of light from the day sky into a night full of stars.

One thing I love about walks is that you are constantly being reminded of things. Also, you see dogs. Today a poodle was in a compromising position, her owner behind her with a plastic bag at the ready. Gabby saw that dog across the street and started barking at her, never mind my mildish reprimands. ("Gabby, stop! That's a nice dog. That dog is so nice. And she speaks French!") The poodle didn't know what to do. So she did the sensible thing. She finished up in dignified silence and then gave it right back to Gabby, who promptly turned away, put her neck fur back down, and trotted off toward the playground like nothing had happened.

Walking Away the Blues

There are times when the blues encroach, for reasons that are not always clear. I was feeling a little sad and anxious this morning, and so I decided to go for a walk. I confess that I doubted being outside would do much good today. It's been so cold and gray. I'm so tired of my gloves and my hood and my boots. But. When I got outside I saw that spring had leaped up from the mat of the boxing ring on the count of nine to deliver a knock-out punch to winter. The sun was warm. The wind was....not brutal. The snow had all melted away.

About ten yards from my house, a cardinal landed on a branch just over my head. He whistled, I whistled back, he whistled back....I am such a great lover of cardinals that I have learned to translate their whistles, and I am privileged to share with you the content of our conversation:

Me: *Oh, hi, there! Oh, my. You're a really pretty one.*
C: *I know. Listen, I need to talk to you about something.*
Me: *I'll bet I know what it is. The seed I keep for you guys on my front porch?*
C: *You mean, the* missing *seed?*
Me: *A squirrel got it. I saw him. He was eating everything with both hands. And when I knocked on the window at him, he laughed at me. But then I opened the door and said* go away *and he did.*
C: *And then....?*
Me: *I know. I have to put more out. I'll do it when I get home.*

The cardinal hung around a while longer, a long time, in fact, and I was thinking, I have never in my life walked away from a cardinal who is right in front of me, but I might have to now. But then he heard another cardinal calling and he flew off and I continued on my walk, which already was lifting my spirits.

I saw a grouping of pale blue flowers on someone's lawn, very pretty, then another stand of the same flowers, only in cobalt blue. I wish I knew their name. Maybe Siberian Squill?

I saw a long tree branch, still bare, extending far out, and its outline looked like a bent-over old lady with one hand on her back, admonishing the lawn below. I could almost see her housedress and her cardigan sweater and her glasses on a chain. Inside her house, a dial telephone on a doily on a telephone table, room for the white and yellow pages in the slot below. Oh, if only there was such a woman I could visit every day! I might be able to use her phone!

I saw sloppy squirrels' nests and the meticulously built nests of birds that transform dental floss and dryer lint and bits of cellophane into works of domestic art.

On the playground by the school, I saw children running around at their usual breakneck speed. One girl had an extravagant pink ribbon clipped in her curly black hair. Another girl had flung her coat to the ground and her bare arms beneath her tank top were exposed. A little boy who stood between them didn't know which way to look. The sounds of children shouting on a playground are oil to the crankcase, I'll tell you. One boy was shouting, "We need two people, two people!" Another boy was practicing dance moves in between tossing a ball back and forth.

I walked on and Gabby's tail wagged like a metronome.

Just as I turned the corner that would lead back toward home, I passed a woman holding her jacket and she indicated the day with a raised chin and said, "Fi*nally*, right?"

"I know," I said. "I just now put my hood down!"

So. When I went passed the monkey bars at the toddler's playground, I saw a young mother instructing her child on the art of ascension. She said, "Just raise your arms, and put your foot right here, and pull up." I'll take that as a metaphor, as a reminder that I am a grateful recipient of all the simple gifts the world has to offer daily, irrespective of anything else going on.

I am going to take myself out to lunch and then I am going to work on my next novel. I'm at a part where I'm talking about lilacs, so you can just imagine.

Spring!

The early-blooming flowers have come to the party, but they still have their coats draped over their shoulders. In small groups, they speak quietly amongst themselves, saying, "Wait. This is April, right?" What with the prospect of snow in the forecast, they are justified in asking the question.

Still, signs of spring abound. Cardinals and robins and sparrows and chickadees flit cheerfully about. Some lawns (not mine, I rush to add) have been raked and cleaned and wait for further transformation. On my walk with Gabby this morning, I saw a clubhouse that had been built for a kid, a new addition to the neighborhood. The occupant had already moved in: I saw a few toys scattered around, and I hoped there were books there, too. I had a deep longing to go and sit in there and eat some Oreos (after carefully separating them, of course), and speculate on what kinds of adventures the day might hold, but one must wait for an invitation. Alas, I am not holding my breath. I might have to get proactive.

The best thing I saw was a "road" drawn on the sidewalk, which ran the length of several houses. It was done in pastel colors of blue and pink chalk, and clearly delineated two narrow lanes. The civic engineer made many, many arrows reminding drivers what direction one was meant to go in, and at the tight U-turn at the end of his road had written a stern, "SLOW DOWN." There was one orange line drawn across the road about half way down, and I thought it might be the place where you were meant to stop and look out for any people or creatures who might want to cross.

It all brought back memories of how much fun it used to be to create such things, how any kid who was in any spontaneously formed group could weigh in about how they thought things should go. If a good idea were offered, there would be a chorus of high, excited "*Yeahs*!" and immediate action. Would that Congress would exhibit such behavior. Would that they would also wear skate keys on a string around their necks, and sport Kool-Aid stains around their mouths. It would make me like them better.

Lost Things

Apparently March has lost its mind and thinks it's January. "In the thirties," said the weather person, "but it feels like the twenties." Wrong. It feels like the minus twenties.

So of course what I am doing is cooking. And I decided that I would make Salisbury Steak, mashed potatoes (baby Yukons, unpeeled, cream and butter and salt and pepper, oh yes) and roasted asparagus with olive oil, salt, pepper, parmesan cheese, and lemon.

I was pretty excited, because that Salisbury steak recipe I have is great—simple, but very good. I sat at my kitchen table with my binder with all the good recipes I've collected over the years and flipped to the main dish section in search of the Salisbury steak recipe. Not there. Not there! I searched again, then once more. Not there.

I did what you might expect. I went online and found a whole bunch of recipes for Salisbury steak, combined the two I liked best, and made dinner. When I sat down to eat, I was disappointed. Naturally it's because I now believe that the recipe I lost was so much better than any recipe I found or ever could find. *Infinitely* better. But here's the truth. If someone made my recipe for me and presented it to me, I'd taste it and say, "Oh. Well, I guess it's not *that* much better." Isn't that the way of lost things?

I saw a documentary once, about the guy whose job it was to make sure that all the clocks in the White House were exactly to-the-minute on time. He showed the interviewer some of his charges, big stately grandfather clocks among them—those were my favorites. The man was soft-spoken but clearly so proud of what he did. At one point, he said something about the possibility of something happening, and the President might look over at one of the clocks and take note of the time.

"You can just imagine...." he said, meaning that if the President looked at a clock, it had better be right.

He took his job so seriously. He endeavored to do it so well. He knew he was only one person on a huge staff, but the job given to him was one he did with honor and integrity and his whole heart. I think of that man now, the reverence he felt for the place he worked, and I just want to weep.

Flower Power

I just shared a little video of lilacs. I love all kinds of flowers, but lilacs are the ones that make me nearly weak-kneed. I have an old, old tree in my back yard still producing those big purple blossoms, and one day a year I go out and harvest them and put bouquets of lilacs all over my house. And then I rarely leave the house until they are all deader than dead. I also have a bank of tiny Miss Kim lilac bushes running along my front porch and they are such hussies, with their strong, strong scent; and when they bloom, I lie on the porch and close my eyes and breathe in and make myself olfactory drunk at every opportunity.

But the best lilac memory I have is this one: I was a freshman in college, living in a dorm—Sanford Tower, University of Minnesota. I happened to mention to a boy I was dating that I loved lilacs. I confess that in the back of my brain I was kind of hoping he'd show up at my room with a little bouquet which I would put on my desk. I could have plucked my own bouquet, but: boys bringing girls flowers, right? Well, he brought me lilacs, just as I'd hoped he would; however, he brought an entire limb of a lilac bush, long as the Mississippi. He showed up at my dorm dragging the thing behind him, grinning.

"Where did you *get* that?" I asked, as though it might have come from a drive-through restaurant or a tire dealership.

Oh, they were spectacular, those lilacs. First place in the land of flower memories (though it must be said I did regret such a significant loss for the bush. And for the person who owned the bush.)

Second place flower memory concerns my then-boyfriend Joel, who, when I was nineteen, sent me a dozen dark red roses wrapped in green tissue and placed in a long white satiny box with a wide red ribbon tied around it. And inside was a card that said I love you. This was in 1967, when long-stemmed red roses cost a pretty penny. I was living in a tiny apartment where my roommate and I shared a bathroom with the four boys who lived in the apartment next door. (You want to know some bathroom stories? Oh, some time I'll tell you some bathroom stories. Okay, just one: Aaron, one of the boys who lived there, lounging in the tub and singing loudly, *Beautiful girl walk a little slower when you walk byyyyyy me....*)

Our furniture was so shabby; the whole house where the apartment was, was ready to fall down with one puff from the big bad wolf. But here came those flowers. And they were so beautiful I didn't know what to do. So after I spun around in a circle, my hands pressed up against my mouth, I left the flowers in the box, because they looked so beautiful there. They darkened, then blackened and died. And in death they were beautiful still, and I kept that box of fragile black roses for a long, long time.

Hope

March is such a tedious month. A month of dirt and gray grass and weather that is always colder than you want it to be. We need spring desperately at this time of year, and March is the guy in the guardhouse wearing sunglasses and a tan uniform, wanting to search your car endlessly before he'll let you pass over the border into Warm Land.

However. March though it is, yesterday I walked Gabigail Starletta Buttons to the school yard and there was a robin convention. Boy, I could have made enough to retire on if I could have opened a worm stand. But there they were, singing their hearts out, hopping on the ground, forming circles like they were organizing soccer teams, lining up on the tree limbs and telephone wires. And two little sparrows took a bath in a puddle and let me watch. Sometimes hope comes in the smallest and most charming and unexpected of ways. For me, that's the hope that sticks.

The Pretend Knitter

This essay appeared in the book "Knitting Yarns: Writers on Knitting." Edited by Ann Hood. Norton & Company, Inc., W. W., 2013.

Can someone who loves everything about knitting— the yarn, the tools of the trade, the knitted projects— actually learn to knit?

Oh, I go to knitting stores where I take a very long time to look at everything. "Can I help you?" some helpful person always asks, and I always say, "No thanks, just looking," in a very busy, maybe even slightly hostile way so that she won't come over and expose me for the pretender that I am.

I go to knitting stores because I wish I were a knitter. I like the colors and textures of the yarn, the brushed suri that is a blend of bamboo and merino and comes in turquoise and brick red colors and the softest shade of pink you ever saw, it's like white blushing. I like the alpaca silk and the sparkle yarns, the worsted wool and copper metallics and super-wash merinos, the aran cotton blends, the silk and angora blends, the Harvest Fields brand in colors of mulberry and olive. I think about buying skeins of yarn to put around my house in baskets like practical bouquets. I think about using the yarns that are fat as the rope clotheslines of yore to wrap big presents, and the yarns so thin they could double as dental floss to wrap little tiny presents. And sometimes I buy them to do just that.

It's not just the yarns I like to look at in

knitting stores. I also enjoy looking at tools of the trade: carrying cases, repair hooks, gauges, tape measures and stitch counters and markers and needles made of bamboo or the Signature needles, made of finest steel. There are circular needles and double-pointed needles and there are cases for holding them. I like the whimsical things: all manner of buttons for putting on a sweater, a wineglass with levels marked off for pouring: a line for lace knitting at the bottom, where you'd get the least amount, then pro-gressing upward to Fair Isle, stockinette stitch, and finally ripping out, and the line marked here assures that you get a full glass of wine indeed.

I look with envy at the beautiful finished products on display: sweaters and hats and mittens and ruffled rose scarves and throws and toys for young children—elephants and teddy bears and rabbits and Uglys. There's a long wooden table with ladder-back chairs in the knitting store in my town, and one of the chairs is all decked out in . . . guess what? Knitting! I like to sit at that table and hear the advice given to this woman making a gunmetal gray pullover, to that one making a shawl. I like the quietly industrious sound of the needles, of the low chatter of women who come not for advice at all but for the camaraderie. On the card that lists the hours for the store I go to is a friendly invitation: *Come knit anytime!* I would like to come and sit and knit, but I had a traumatic knitting experience. Think of it as having hit the bottom of the pool at my first diving lesson.

I grew up an army brat, and when I was a little kid, in the years 1951-54, we were stationed in Germany. While we were there, the postwar economy made it possible for us to have the luxury of a full-time maid. Gerti was her name. She was a curly brown-haired woman whom I recall as having a pleasing constellation of moles on one side of her face and an equally pleasing disposition. She had no problem with me following her around as she did her chores, lying at her feet when she ironed, or sitting practically on top of her when she knitted. She was a skilled knitter, Gerti, and I was mesmerized by the flash of her needles, the finished products ever emerging from them, and most of all, the way she rarely even looked at what she was doing. It was all in the attitude, I decided, and I tried to knit using attitude, which was just about as successful as you might think it would be. Gerti did manage to teach me to cast on, and she taught me a simple garter stitch, and I never forgot it. But what could you do with *that?* I wanted to be a knitter extraordinaire: I had visions of making sweaters like my Aunt Kate sent me every Christmas, my favorite being a navy blue one that featured a clown holding balloons. I wanted to make soft pink and blue and yellow baby blankets and hats and mittens and socks that would make the recipients go all soft in the eyes. But in all the ensuing years after Gerti taught me the garter stitch, all I ever knit were scarves of varying widths, full of holes from dropped stitches because I didn't know how to fix dropped stitches. Finally, I gave up.

But then when I was a sophomore in college, I lived with a woman named Lois whom I adored. We had no money but we had our guitars and our cowgirl boots and our Boone's Farm wine and our boyfriends and we had *fun*. I got it in mind, one winter, to knit her a scarf. It would work this time; it would be beautiful. And it would be warm, which, in Minnesota moves right past being a blessing into the territory of survival.

Lois's eyes were a rich brown color, and so I endeavored to find a shade of yarn I thought would match. I came pretty close, and I bought several skeins and a pair of needles and hid them away. When she wasn't around, I worked on her scarf. Garter stitch, of course. And soon there were the usual dropped stitches, which I thought could be made up for by making the scarf long. Very long. Then longer. Then perhaps a bit too long. No. Not perhaps. Definitely too long. It looked like something you might give someone to tie around a bedpost and then use to escape a burning building. And here is my tip given to all knitters everywhere: making something longer does not make up for dropped stitches. Rather, it accentuates them.

Next problem: I had forgotten how to cast off. But I did it, eventually, and then I used the yard I had left to make some fringe, which was not lush and attractive but thin, like a near-bald man's remaining hair raked hopefully over the top of his head. Or, more accurately, like the cilia on a paramecium, if you've ever had the good fortune to see a paramecium, and if you have not, I invite you to Google "paramecium" right now and you will have a very good idea of what my friend's scarf fringe looked like. And that wasn't even the worst of it. Somehow the thing had gotten really crooked, so it went first to the left, then to the right in really a rather hectic way, as though the scarf was having an argument with itself about which was the right way to get *out* of there.

Well. I held my gift up before me and I just wanted to weep. Never had such glorious intentions come to such a sorry end. I had wanted to give my friend a gift not only from my heart but from my hands, I had wanted to make her something that made her full of gratitude, and all I had made was a mess, even by the most lenient of standards. Nonetheless, I presented it to her the next day with a thousand and one excuses. She lifted the scarf from the box and gamely wrapped it around her neck. And wrapped it around some more, and then some more, which, if you've been paying attention to this story, you'd know she would have had to do in order not to trip on it. She stood beneath the kitchen overhead light—one of the few lights in the apartment that worked—to show me how it looked. And then, as if I had not suffered enough humiliation, I saw that the color was not a deep and rich brown, but rather a color like something you take Imodium for.

I shrugged. I said, "I'm sorry." I said, "I wanted to give you something that I made." And you know what she said? She said, "But you did.

And I love it."

She did indeed seem to love it. The next day, she wrapped the scarf around her neck where it peeked odiously out from the top of her rather nice winter coat. She wore it that day and the next and the next. She wore it all winter. For all I know, she still has it. I would ask her, but I'm embarrassed to.

But here's the thing. The lesson in all this, which I did not learn then, is that so much of the joy of knitting is not in the creation of a perfect product. Rather, it is in the act of using one's own bodily skills to make something for someone else's body. The gift is not so much in the end result (although the end results are often if not usually spectacular), but in the way that something made with one own hands says a few things of utmost importance:

I made this for you.

I thought of you while I made it.

I guess I kind of love you.

Last time I was busily browsing in my local store, this time venturing to say, "What's *this?*" and then exclaiming over its beauty, or ingenuity or sly humor, the owner, whose name is Sue, said, "You know, you really should learn to knit."

Busted. But oh so happily. I said, "I know," and I got a schedule of classes. "But I'm not taking a class in the summer," I told her. "I'm taking it in the *winter,* that's when *I'm* doing it," I said And Sue said, *"0-kay."*

I don't think I've ever said this before, but I can't wait for winter.

Lemon Kerfuffle

Well. If this dessert didn't make me want to put on my rhinestone cat-eye glasses and a nice print house dress, and put Dinah Shore and Perry Como on the stereo. I mean that in the very best of ways ("Would you like to swing on a star, carry moonbeams home in a jar?" I mean, jeez who wouldn't?).

Those who know me are aware of my constant longing to step in the time machine and come out when IPhones were not even a gleam in anyone's eye. (I think I have to write a short story collection called, The Day I Murdered My Electronics and Then Had a Party to Which No One Was Invited by Evite.)

Anyway, this wonderful old-fashioned recipe was sent to me by the wonderful Karen Schneider, and I tried it today and it is all I want for dinner. However, I also made a chicken pot pie so I'm going to have a tablespoon of that and then a *bunch* of this.

Aunt Marion's Lemon Sponge Pudding aka Lemon Kerfuffle 6 servings

3 T. butter, softened
1 c. sugar
1/8 t. salt
4 large eggs, at room temperature and separated
3 T. flour
1/3 c. lemon juice (1 large lemon)
1 T. grated lemon zest
1 c. whole milk
Berries for garnish (optional)

1. Preheat oven to 325 degrees. Lightly butter a 2-quart round casserole, a 9-inch cake pan, or six 6-ounce ramekins.

2. Use a wooden spoon to combine butter, sugar, and salt in a mixing bowl. With a mixer, beat in egg yolks. Stir in flour, lemon juice and zest. Add milk and mix thoroughly.

3. In a separate bowl, beat egg whites until stiff but still moist. Gently whisk the whites into the lemon batter, just blending until no large lumps of egg white remain. (This is where the mixture looks strange—you'll want to keep whisking to make it smooth, but don't do it!)

4. Spoon the batter into the baking dish(es). Bake in a water bath* until a knife inserted in the center comes out clean, 30-50 minutes. Let stand for 10 more minutes in its "tub." Serve warm, at room temperature, or chilled.

*Water bath: Use a pan large enough to accommodate your pudding dish so it doesn't touch the pan's sides. Place a metal rack or a folded towel on the bottom of the pan so the dish doesn't touch the pan's bottom. Put the baking dish in the pan then pour enough very hot water into the pan so the water level is halfway up the sides of the baking dish. Be careful to not get any water into the pudding!

Little Teachers

I was once reading to my then three-year-old grandson Matthew, the two of us sitting in a big chair together, a book my mother gave to me when I was a child: *Bertram and his Fabulous Animals*. We were reading a part that scares Matthew, but he likes to read that part again and again.

The situation is that Bertram is in the attic looking for the troublesome Squeazle Weasel, who has escaped Bertram and gone in between the walls, where he makes scrabbling sounds and high-pitched squeals, scaring the family to death. So Bertram is up there all alone in the attic, and it's beginning to get dark, and he is feeling afraid. As is Matthew, sitting beside me with his eyes wide. But this time when I read the section to him, he says, "I wish Bertram could come out of this story and go upstairs and get my flashlight and then come back into the story." I say, "What a great idea," and we sat quietly for a moment together, imagining this. But the problem with stories is that if the problem goes away, the story does, too. Thus Bertram stands shivering in the attic, and we readers shiver along with him. And although we may be uncom-fortable, we are very satisfied, too. Thus Matthew saying, "No, just read the part about the attic," again and again and again. Finally, though, I say, "Okay, but then we're going to read another story."

Matthew is quiet.

"It's about a dinosaur egg Bertram and his friend Ginny are going to hatch."

"Well...." Matthew says.

"Shall we read just a few paragraphs?" I say, and he nods yes and settles back in the chair. And I think again: shouldn't I just move here?

Here is what Matthew the three-year-old therapist taught me: When something scares you, you revisit it over and over until a solution comes to you. Here's what else he taught me: you must have faith that a solution will come, or you'll never make the effort to find it. And here is what two-year-old Katelyn taught me: A fine way to get dressed in the morning is to put on tights, a dress, a shirt over the dress, a backpack holding stuffed animals, a hat, butterfly wings, and many bracelets. I may try it. I'm not so far from trying it.

Last time my friend Phyllis visited me, she said, "Don't you ever comb your hair?"

"I forget," I told her.

Time of Accounting

When I was a young girl, I took very seriously the tenets of my Catholic faith. I believed in everything: innocent-eyed babies in limbo, whom I always pictured as kicking their chubby little legs as they lay on pink and blue infused clouds. I believed in the poor souls in purgatory, the writhing sinners in hell, the floating angels who had made it to heaven and presumably got to do all kinds of fun things, though I never was very clear on what those things were. Playing harp? Nonetheless, I was keenly focused on avoiding hell and purgatory both, and I worried a lot about what my sins were or could be. It seemed there was a lot of slipperiness involved: could a venial sin slide right into mortal? Was there unintended sin that still counted as a big black mark in the book of reckoning? I used to wish for a bracelet I could wear, a pretty gold band that would give me a little shock every time I was about to do something wrong. Of course, that is what a conscience does, but I didn't quite trust my conscience. I wanted something more objective, and it seemed to me that gold bracelet would put any ambiguity to rest. *ZZZT!* You're sinning! Stop immediately!

In a related vein, I have always had a romantic notion that upon one's deathbed, one could at last do a serious accounting, a balancing out of the good one did versus the not-so-good. This would lead to a realistic tally of the worth of one's time upon the earth, and, by extension, point to where you might be expected to go after you took your last breath.

Here's what I think now. I am no longer a practicing Catholic, though I do appreciate the calm that can descend upon sitting in a beautiful Catholic church, especially an empty one. I see that the gold bracelet was a way of avoiding my responsibility to know right from wrong, that the onus was on me to pay attention to what a deep and true inner voice was telling me.

The children of Parkland—and of this entire nation—are taking up a cause to achieve a goal that we adults have failed to achieve. I am so proud of these children. I am so inspired by them. I think that where we have failed, they might very well succeed.

But here's the problem. They are children. Sensitive, articulate and intelligent as they may be, they are only high school students and they are being robbed of a kind of innocence and even ignorance that should be theirs to enjoy. It is not yet time for them to shoulder problems of this magnitude. One young woman talked about how she had been planning a prom theme; now she's suggesting kevlar vests and bulletproof walls in school. Another, contemplating the fact that she too could have been killed, said, "I'm fourteen. I haven't even driven a car yet."

I honor the fact that these kids are being politicized and respect the fact that they are turning their anguish into action, but will they never just get to act like the children that they are?

Nothing is going to erase what happened to them. And I hope that the rage and the activism continues until we cut off the head of the snake and ban assault weapons.

I see suddenly and quite clearly that the time of accounting is not when you are on your death bed, but rather when you are walking through life. Each day you can listen to your conscience or avoid it. Each day you can dip your fingers into a font of a particular kind of holy water and make a sign that you're ready to face the truth. For me, it comes to acknowledging this: We have failed these children, so that they are having to take matters into their own hands. The least we can do is join them, in whatever way we can. I am proud to, and broken-hearted.

Flu

Count me as another one enduring a horrible flu that's going around. Lucky for me I have good medicine: a get-well card from Phyllis; Miss Gabby, registered dog nurse, who comforts with her very presence, as dogs do whether you're sick, well, or in between; also Bill, who offers a lot of help, too. For example, I showed him one of the poems in Billy Collins' new book and he said, "Why can't all poetry be like this?" Also, my friend Pam, who is delivering some bone broth. I expect to fly around like superman after I drink that. In the meantime, I think I'll take my 34th nap of the day now.

My Winter Day

Look out the front door window, look out the back.
Pace around a little. Look out some more windows,
where the icicles have gotten even longer. Think:
I'm not going out. It's too cold! Look at Gabby, who
is looking hopefully up at me. I decide I'll take her
for a walk and test out the weather.

Well, it's cold, but the sun is so warm. And the
snow is sparkling. And the little kids are out for
recess on the playground, and there is that joyful
mix of shouting and yelling. One girl sits on the
bench like Queen Victoria and her two little friends
seem to be trying to court her. One boy, wearing
pink glasses, stands stock still and open-mouthed,
with his hood fallen off his head, daydreaming—a
future Bill Gates, I'll bet. A bunch of boys have built
a little snow hill that they are sliding down and in
their imaginations. I'll bet they see that hill as a
mountain. Another group of kids is rolling a ball to
be the head of a snowman. A snow fort might be in
progress. Kids on the monkey bars. Kids on the
swings. Mittens, pom-poms on knit hats, all those
puffy jackets and all those boots. Soon the kids will
march back into the classroom and their cheeks
will be rosy and their energy level will be back up.
Way up. And maybe the teachers will sigh and look
at their watches.

I drop Gabby off at home and keep going. I'm
going to walk into town and go to the library and
then go to the bank and then, whoops! to Five Guys
for a hamburger. This is because of the conversation I had with a Lyft driver last night. He drove me

back from downtown and the whole way we talked about food. He talked most about chocolate malts and this made hamburgers start floating in my mind like they did in Wimpy's.

So I walk along and I look in all the store windows and watch people. Some people are bundled up like me—I'm wearing my dopey hat that ties beneath my chin (but oh it's warm!) and no makeup and my hair is a mess and I'm hoping I don't run into anyone I know.

At the bank, there is a woman in a wheelchair carrying a pink plastic shovel on her lap (to remove snow when she has to?) and over her winter jacket is a blanket with a Christmas theme. She is yelling at an employee. Something about how that employee is no help at all. Then the woman says, "Can I see a manger, please? Can I see a manager? *Hello?* Can I see a manager, is there a *manager*?" And then she's yelling really loud, nearly crying. All of us in line are kind of looking at each other and then away. I say to the woman ahead of me, "Maybe the moon is doing something weird." "I think it is," she says. "Everywhere I go today, something strange is happening."

I know the woman is making a terrible fuss, but I wonder if she isn't entitled to it. I wonder if she has to fight for her rights all the time. I wonder if she is so tired of being overlooked, ignored, put second. I remember a man who was a friend of mine and a brilliant writer who was wheelchair bound and he wanted to see a movie and he was told there was no access seating. So he picked another movie. And the friend who was with him said, "No. You don't have to settle," and she made some kind of arrangement to get him in anyway.

Well, the employee who came out in the bank spoke quite reasonably and kindly to the angry woman, who immediately calmed down, and everyone felt better.

Next I went to Five Guys and guess who came in? The guy who directed my play of *The Pull of the Moon*! He and his lovely girlfriend, who is an actor. I was so glad to see them, not least because I gave them a good two-thirds of my French fries because I had *way* too many. I was embarrassed because I looked like hell but we had such a good time talking I soon forgot about how bad I looked. When we finished talking and he went up to order, I heard him say, "No, we already have French fries," and I don't know, it just made me happy.

When I was in the library, there was a bulletin board with many pieces of paper tacked up on it that began "Before I die...." and people had filled them out in various ways. Fascinating, and it is a privilege of my free-form occupation that I had time to read them all. Some were hopeful. Some were bitter. Some seemed full of sadness. Some were funny, as in "I want to eat all the food I can and get a cat." These pieces of paper gave me an idea for a short story collection.

When I came home, I took a nap, and when I woke up, I had an idea for a novel.

I've told a few people that *Night of Miracles*, my next book coming out in November, will be my last. All the ideas I've had seem lackluster, like they're hanging around in their bathrobes and staring into space and smoking. But all of a sudden, a little light is lit.

I was going to go to Florida to visit a friend and get warm. Because of the icicles, which are now even longer, as you can see in the photo. But then I saw a snowman. And also I got an idea.

You never know what will happen in the course of the day, except you know that Gabby will get fed twice. Here I go to feed her now.

Gabby: It's about time. Do you know how early Bill fed me this morning? I'm starving! Plus when are we getting another dog?

How I De-cluttered My House in 1-1/2 Minutes

I stood in my sewing room, looking at all the shelves of fabric. All the overstuffed shelves of fabric. (This was after having seen the overstuffed cupboards in the kitchen, my overstuffed desk drawers, my over-stuffed closet where tops are saying "Move *over*!" to each other, my chaotic "wrapping station" where it looks like an explosion happened that sent ribbons and happy birthday paper and wine gift bags flying.)

Anyway, I stood in the sewing room, thinking, all right, I'm getting rid of half this fabric. I'm giving it away. I don't need all this! Then I got a little headache and stomach ache at the same time plus I remembered a time I gave stuff away and then what happened? Bam! The next day, I *needed* it.

So I said the hell with it, and went upstairs to have a nice cup of coffee. Done.

When I die, my children can get a bulldozer and have at it. Until then, I've got stuff. And I'm keeping it. If you think having five cupcake pans is nuts, well, then, I'm nuts. (One pan for extra large, two for regular, two for mini.)

P.S. "When I die" puts me in mind of my friend Warren Nelson's song that begins, "When I die/Don't put me in the ground/Put my ashes in the ashtray/And drive me around."

This is what I would call a good attitude.

P.P.S. Another snowy day and the icicles hang long off my roof. They are extraordinary. Natural wonders. If I had any spirit at all, I'd reach out the window and break one off and suck on it.

Speaking of spirit, I miss the girl I was at nineteen who, one night just after Christmas time, walked with my roommate to a bridge over the Mississippi River. We were dragging our Christmas tree behind us because we wanted to give it a Viking funeral. We set it on fire and dropped it in the river. I believe we were wearing pajamas under our winter coats.

Those were the days. Those were the days when my friend Ron once called in the middle of the night and said, "Come over." I said, "It's the middle of the night!" He said, "If you're good people, you'll come over." I did. I took the car my roommate and I had just bought together even though I had no driver's license. (Also no money, but you know.) It was a '66 burgundy Mustang convertible with a white interior (I know, I should have kept it). Anyway, I didn't know how to work the defroster so I lowered the top and sat on top of the driver's seat so I could see over the windshield to drive. Luckily, no cop stopped me. I had a good time at Ron's. For one thing, there was good music playing (the Beatles) and for another, I got to sit under the quilt his grandmother made him.

I am happy to say that if certain people called me in the middle of the night these days to say, "Come over." I would do it. Luckily, I now have a driver's license and a car where I can work the defroster. More or less.

And now, if you'll excuse me, I'm going to make valentines. At least one. Should you make a valentine? If you do, I can tell you that whoever gets it will be very pleased, even if it's crummy, and believe me, my valentine(s) will be crummy. But heartfelt! Such a joy to look in your mailbox and find something that is not a bill. It's like finding dinosaur bones in your back yard.

Fabric Love

Yesterday I pulled a vintage kimono from my closet that I bought over twenty years ago and that has been hanging there since. I thought, why don't I make a jacket of this, and wear it? The problem was, it would mean cutting off the beautiful hanging-down part of the kimono sleeves. I wouldn't do it. I couldn't do it. Instead, I brought it to my favorite dry cleaner/alteration shop. The woman who owns the place and I hovered over the kimono for many long minutes, admiring the fabric and the hand sewing. Then she pointed to the floral design and said, "This is hand-painted." "Really?" I said. Then we had to look some more.

I told the woman what I wanted to do, and after we talked about the various pros and cons of framing the thing, she agreed that the kimono would make a lovely jacket. I told her I was afraid to cut it, she said, "Me, too!"

"Oh jeez," I said, "don't tell me that!" We looked longer at the kimono and then she said, "You know what? I think this is reversible. Try it on."

"*You* try it on so I can look at you in it," I said. She smiled, took off her down vest and slipped on the kimono, now turned inside out, and regarded herself in the mirror. And yes, it was reversible, she'd just have to blind hem everything after she cut it. She put safety pins in place for where she'd have to cut. Then, "I'm going in the back," she said ominously, and there were scissors in her eyes.

I ran toward the door, saying, "I'm so nervous!" She went toward the back of the store, saying, "Me, too!"

On Thursday, I'll pick it up. I hope I did the right thing.

You know what was the best thing about that experience? The friendly, woman-to-woman exchange I had with another fabric lover. The way the sun poured into the store. The shine of the safety pins as she carefully put them in place, and the shape of her fingers—she's an older woman with beautiful hands. The way the dry-cleaned clothes on the rack behind her almost seemed to be looking over the woman's shoulder to see this exotic newcomer that lay vastly appreciated on the counter before us humans even as we planned for it a little bit of doom.

The Palmer House

I suppose something a lot of people believe is that life rarely turns out the way you think it will. That the fantasies you enjoy as a child are just that, fantasies. But let me tell you something. Every time I sit in the lobby of the Palmer House, I feel like I used to when I was a little girl and stuck a cocktail umbrella into my juice and thought, someday I'm going to sit in a fancy place and have a fancy drink just like this one.

Well, the drink I had at The Palmer House the other day was mint hot chocolate, because the temperature was three thousand degrees below zero. But oh, that atmosphere. It never fails to inspire. Sorry the photo is so bad. But you get the idea. Can you imagine anyone building something like that today? I mean, you'd have to email into the past and get Michelangelo.

Bye-Bye

Someone just posted "When you leave your pets do you say, "I'll be back soon," or is that just me?

I don't say that. Here's what I say: "Oh, sweetie, I'm so sorry. We're going out now, and you can't come this time. You can come next time. But right now we're just going to a play and then we'll be *right back*. Okay? And when we come back you get another walk, okay? One where you get to choose the route, you like that. You be a good girl and guard the house. And you can play with Gracie. And you can look out the window and I'll bet you'll see a *dog* walking by, won't that be nice? There's fresh water in your bowl. And you had a nice dinner, didn't you? You can lie in your bed if you want. Do you want the radio on? Let's turn the radio on for you. You want NPR? Or classical? Oh, I know, I could put on Animal Planet on the TV for you! But sometimes that's violent. Never mind. Okay, going now. Come over here and I'll pet you a little before I go."

And then the play is over.

Gabigail Starletta Buttons

Did you ever see a beautiful person admiring themselves in a mirror or in a storefront reflection It must be hard not to when you're so very good looking. But all my admiration goes to the ones who are really, really beautiful and care not one whit how they look. I give you the majestic Gabigail Starletta Buttons:

Winter Soup

When really cold weather comes, I understand fully and completely the word "dart." It's how I move all the time, outside, darting here and there. I feel like the director of a film has said, "Okay, now act like you're *making a break for it!*"

I am not a fan of the cold, never mind that my grandma, Frieda Loney, tried to convince me that it was "refreshing." I'll tell you what's refreshing: an ice cold martini with a good friend at a really fun restaurant, that's what's refreshing.

But I must admit that cold weather is not all bad. When it's here, I feel no guilt about lying under vintage quilts and watching old movies while I sip hot wassail. I enjoy the smell of all kinds of things baking in the oven, from roasted chicken to chocolate cake to barbecued ribs. And soup, oh, soup! This is the season for soup! Yesterday, I made white bean soup. Today, I'm trying one I haven't made before.

First, put on some country and western music, like Bob Wills and his Texas Playboys (optional). Put on an apron (also optional, but you'll never convince me that wearing an apron doesn't make things turn out better)

Make sure the dog has fresh water. If you don't have a dog, you really ought to get one.

Seared Broccoli and Potato Soup
6 servings
From New York Times Cooking

½ c. olive oil, plus more as needed
2 heads broccoli (about 2 lbs), separated into small
    florets, stems peeled and diced
2 ½ t. kosher salt, more to taste
2 T. unsalted butter
1 large Spanish onion, diced
5 cloves garlic, chopped
½ t. black pepper, more for finishing
¼ t. red pepper flakes
½ lb. potatoes, peeled and thinly sliced
¼ t. finely grated lemon zest
1½ T. fresh lemon juice, more to taste
 Grated Parmesan, to finish
 Flaky sea salt, to finish

1. In a large soup pot, heat 2 tablespoons of oil over
high heat. Add about a third of the broccoli, just enough
so that it covers the bottom of the pan in a single layer
without overcrowding. Cook broccoli without moving it
for about 3 to 4 minutes, or until dark brown on one
side only (leave the other side bright green). Transfer to
a big bowl and repeat with remaining broccoli and more
oil. When all the broccoli has been browned, season
with 1 teaspoon salt and set aside.

2. Reduce heat to medium-low. Add butter and
remaining 2 tablespoons of oil to pan. Add onions and
garlic, black and red peppers, and 1/2 teaspoon salt.
Cook onion-garlic mixture until soft and translucent,
about 4 minutes. Add potato to the pot with 1 quart
water and remaining 1 teaspoon salt. Bring to a simmer,
cover pot and cook until potato is just tender, 10 to 15

minutes. Add broccoli, cover again and cook until tender, another 5 to 10 minutes.

3. Add lemon zest and roughly purée soup with an immersion or regular blender, leaving some small chunks for texture. Stir in lemon juice. Finish with grated Parmesan, a drizzle of olive oil, black pepper and flaky sea salt.

While you eat, ask anyone if they've ever heard this wonderful Emily Dickinson quote from one of her letters: *I hope you love birds, too. It is economical. It saves going to heaven.*

The Year I Ruined Christmas

Here's a Christmas essay for you. If you want to read it, I recommend that you pour a glass of wine, or a mug of hot chocolate, and put your feet up! Merry Christmas, everyone.

As a child, I saw my mother prepare for Christmas every year, and it never occurred to me that labor was involved. I thought it was my mother's joy and privilege to hang tinsel on the tree strand by strand, to make sure that every room in the house had a touch of Christmas, down to the Santa-themed rug and hand towels in the bathroom. She would sit at a card table night after night to carefully and creatively wrap gifts, she baked hundreds of Christmas cookies, hand-wrote messages on Christmas cards that went near and far, and she planned, shopped for and served a Christmas dinner that was nearly unbearably delicious: turkey, stuffing, green bean bake, sweet potatoes, mashed potatoes, reception salad, cucumbers in sour cream, rolls and butter, and cranberry sauce that in later years, courtesy of Susan Stamford, got fancied up.

I always wanted to drink the gravy my mom made right out of the boat. (And if there was any left after dinner, I did exactly that. And then I used a Parker House roll to scrape up any remains.) For dessert, there were homemade pies and Christmas cookies and chocolates you could pluck out of the king-sized box of Whitman's that my parents bought every year. Oh, that messenger boy!

When I grew up, I realized the truth. My mother prepared for the holidays joyfully, but she also labored mightily. Still, when she was well up into her eighties, she continued doing it. Oh, she lightened her load a little bit: she prepared certain dishes the day ahead, and guests brought some side dishes that she always used to make. But she still did the bulk of the labor, including laying a tablecloth beneath the elegantly set wedding china that was older than I, and guess how many stains were on it? Zero, that's how many, because all her life, up until the day she went into the hospital for the last time, my mother was a laundress extraordinaire. If there were a category in the Olympics for laundry, my mother would have been a gold-medal winner.

Year after year after year, my mother prepared and served and helped clean up after huge holiday dinners. And the woman did not even have a dishwasher until she was 89 years old, when she moved into an independent living apartment, where, ironically, she finally stopped hosting holiday dinners.

After she moved to that apartment, we were on the phone one day. Christmas was a few weeks away, and she told me how much she missed getting Christmas cards. "Nobody sends them anymore," she told me. "Or if they do, they send emails or those preprinted photographs, and that's not the same."

She was right. It wasn't the same as getting all those envelopes in your mailbox, and opening them to find all those different, often glittery images, all those verses written in the card as well as a handwritten note—or even a multi-page letter!—from the person who'd sent it to you. When you got those cards, you understood that this was from someone you knew, who knew you.

My mom used to keep all her Christmas cards in a basket bedecked with red ribbon, and I used to love to look at them all, and read all the letters. All those people, still keeping in touch. I even liked reading the letters from people I didn't know, because it was an honest and reassuring peek into someone else's life. But by the time my mom reached her 90s, many of the people who used to send her cards had died. And the people who were left mostly didn't send cards anymore. I always sent my mom the most beautiful card I could find, and she displayed it like it was a Van Gogh. My sister and brother sent her beautiful cards, too. But that was about it.

So that Christmas, her last Christmas as it turned out, I got an idea. I asked everyone on Facebook to send my mom a "real" Christmas card. I thought she might even get one hundred or so, and wouldn't that be fun? I told my sister, who lives in Minnesota where my Mom lived, and we decided to keep it a secret from my mother.

Several days after I made the request, my mom called me and said, "You know what? I got six Christmas cards in the mail today, and are they ever pretty, and I don't even know these people!"

"Oh, really?" I said, and even though we were on the phone, I fought to disguise my smile.

Well.

By time the experiment was finished, my mom had gotten well over 1,200 cards. My sister had to start opening the envelopes for her because it wore my mom's hands out, slicing open so many envelopes. The cards were arriving in those big plastic mail bins and were delivered straight to her door, since there was no way they'd fit in her mailbox. They came from all over the U.S. and from a few places outside the U.S. And not only did the people send cards, they sent notes along with them: Stories. Memories. Good wishes. Compliments to my mother for being a good writer.

After the cards first started coming, she wrote a thank-you letter that she asked me to post on Facebook and so, for the first time, she was both online and published. (She had always had a dream of being a published writer. In fact, when I became a writer, my father told me, "You got *her* job!") My mother became a minor celebrity in her building.

There was a story done about her in the St. Paul Pioneer Press.

I still have one of those cards that my mom kept with her when she went into hospice. It features three angels shown in a kind of 3-D way. In dim light, you'd swear they were real, and floating in the air for the sake of your consolation. After my mom died, I put the card face out on a bookshelf and if I'm having a bad day, I sit and look at it.

So. When the first Christmas without my mom came around, I felt I needed to do something really special. I invited my out-of-town daughter and her husband and three children to spend the holiday

with me. Also, I invited my son-in-law's mother.
With my other, nearby daughter and her husband
and my partner Bill and me, it would be a full
house. I was thrilled. I wanted to recreate all the
things my mother used to do. And I intended for
everything to be perfect, just as it was when she
did it. I suppose I was hoping to bring her back, at
least in some way.

I decorated the house. Each room had
something: mini Christmas trees or snow globes or
whimsical things like dogs dressed as angels. By
the fireplace was a big basket holding Christmas-
themed books for both children and adults, and in
the TV room, I lined up all the Christmas movies,
including my favorite, "A Christmas Story," which I
could hardly wait for us all to watch together. I
bought tickets to the Joffrey's "The Nutcracker" so
that I could take my three grandchildren to it and
we could all thrill to it snowing on stage.

I wanted to make all the food on Christmas
Day, so that it would be as fresh as possible. The
pies—all homemade, of course, including the
crust—would be made in the early morning.
(Maybe it would snow! I thought. Maybe I would be
rolling out dough while everyone was upstairs
sleeping, and huge, lacy flakes would be beautifully
drifting and Christmas music would be softly
playing and when people got up the coffee would
be ready and they'd sit at the table in their pajamas
and say, "Ohhhh, something smells so good!")

I decided I wouldn't make the white bread and
the cornbread that would be used for stuffing, and I
would buy dinner rolls, that was my only

concession. Otherwise, everything would be made from scratch. (My son-in-law's mom once joked, "When you cook, you make the hydrogen and the oxygen for the water you use.") I figured I would cook my brains out all day and the others could amuse themselves in any way that they wanted: playing games, talking, taking walks in the neighborhood, going downtown, maybe reading together from the big pile of Christmas books.

You see where this is going, no doubt. You know what happens when your expectations are as high as the moon.

Things did not go well. People kind of didn't know what to do. When my sweet granddaughter came in the kitchen and said she wanted to make a pie of her own, I did not delight in this but instead thought, *No No No*, I don't have *time*! She made her little pie, but everything about the experience was off. There was no joy in Mudville.

At one point, when everything was prepared and the turkey was roasting in the oven, I realized how exhausted I was. I truly felt like I was going to keel over. I told Bill I was going to go upstairs and take a nap. And that's what I did. With a houseful of people whom I loved and had invited to spend Christmas with me, I went upstairs to my bedroom and went to sleep. It was like throwing a party, opening the door to the guests and saying, "What the hell are you doing here?"

I will say the food was great. And I will say things marginally improved when my grand-children and I decided to write a play ("The Ugliest Cat at the Shelter") and perform it to an admittedly biased audience of a few relatives who applauded it heartily.

After my guests left, I did a postmortem, and I realized a few things. I am not my mother, and I am not honor-bound to try to do all the things she did in the way that she did them. I don't have the stamina or the patience or the foresight or the skill or even the desire. I am now and forever the one who gets tired easily, who becomes overwhelmed by too many people in the house or too many things to do. And I can't get stains out of anything, not even with OxiClean.

No, I am not my mother. I am deeply, endlessly grateful for what she did and who she was, but I am a different kind of person. And as appreciative as she was of tradition, I think she would be the first to say, "For heaven's sake, you don't have to do what I did!"

There is one way I tried to be like her that I don't regret, though, and that is in trying to bring back the idea of handwritten cards. And I am happy to say that that idea took root in other ways, too. After the experience with my mother, one Facebook friend asked that cards be sent to honor her parent's 75th wedding anniversary; one inspired people to send beautiful cards to nursing homes, to be given to people who rarely if ever got mail. It reminded me of what Christmas is supposed to be about. Good Will. Kindness. Sharing. Wonder. Spontaneity. Generosity. Small but meaningful things that take root in the heart, and blossom, and stay.

Incidentally, the year after the year I ruined Christmas, I went to my daughter's house for Christmas. It was wonderful. I had such a good time I cried.

Gifts

The Christmas I was eight, we were living in
Oklahoma. It was Christmas Eve, which is when we
opened our presents, and my mother was making
me *crazy*. She was in the bathtub, which was
seemingly her favorite place to be, taking a bath
that was lasting so long I though it would be the
new year before she emerged. I lay on the floor of
the hall outside the door, waiting to hear the first
sound that would indicate that she was getting out
of there. Occasionally I called in to remind her that
we were *waiting*......I was so frustrated. Why on
earth would anyone *delay* opening presents?

I know the answer to that question now. So
much of giving a gift is bound up with things other
than the actual moment of presentation. Selecting
something you think the person might love.
Wrapping it. I know a lot of people hate wrapping,
but I love it (I should add that I cannot be in a
hurry). I like to use nice or creative paper (funny
papers, anyone?) and really pretty ribbon and
various do-dads on the packages. I am a big fan of
glitter. I like to imagine how a gift will be received,
I like to think about the recipient wearing it, or
eating it, or using it. As we speak, so to speak, there
are empty boxes on my landing, beautifully
wrapped. Nothing in there, they are just pretty to
look at, and they hint at the anticipation that is
such a wonderful part of this season.

I now understand that my mother didn't
exactly want the anticipation to end. She sat in a
tub of steaming, fragrant water, probably thinking

about the beautiful sight of the presents under the tree, and she no doubt was reviewing what everyone was getting. (She herself often got beautiful negligees which she opened and then immediately slammed the lid of the box back on, as though snakes were trying to escape from it, while my dad sat grinning.)

We don't always succeed at giving someone something they really want or need (I am reminded here of a friend's elderly aunt, who opened a very nice gift he got her, frowned, and said, "Why doesn't anyone ever ask me what I *want*?"). But what I love about gift-giving is the intention of one person to bring joy to another. And the anticipation around that. About the fun of anticipation and about the need to spring- and fall-clean. You were right, Mom. I get it now. And I wish you could somehow know that as I go around looking at things to give people this year, I keep finding things I almost buy for you, before I remember. If there is anything that losing those we love teaches, it's that we are blessed to be with the ones we still have.

Happy holidays to everyone, and thank you for gifting me every day of the year with your open-hearted presence on this page.

The Love of Reading

When I was maybe four years old, my mother gave me the most enchanting book. It was Sleeping Beauty, but a really beautiful version of the story, with many cutouts, and with lots of floating fairies, each more beautiful than the next. The one who captivated me most was the bad fairy, with her raven locks and red dress, with the way she was peeking out from behind a stone column, clearly not wanted at the festivities.

I would go to my room, close the door, sit on the floor and look at those pictures, and tell myself the story as I remembered it from my mother reading it to me. Time held still, then, and I was lost to the merging of author's and reader's imagination, which is what I believe happens when we read. I'm about to go to bed and read again, and I will be just as enchanted as I ever was. I think that reading is the most consistently reliable pleasure we have.

My mother's wish, as she grew older, was that she would never have to stop reading, and she never did. She lost some vision but she had audio tapes even in her hospice room, which is to say that she always had a lot of good company. Funny how i comforts me to remember that, and how the notion of going upstairs to read now feels like even more than it is.

Giving Thanks

In 1988, I wrote an article on Thanksgiving for Parents magazine. Here's an excerpt that still holds true for me. It comes after a part where I talk about how we go around the table and say what we are grateful for.

We finish eating, clean up, and go about our business. We're all too full, but we are happy. I think that feeling full after a good meal can always make you kind of happy, but I think that this particular happiness comes because of our satisfaction in having said right out loud that we love things about our life. If it is a sad commentary on human habits that we don't often enough articulate our gratefulness for what means the most to us, it is a tribute to the human spirit that we have created a holiday that gives us a chance to do just that. I am grateful for the opportunity to be grateful.

I want to thank everyone on this page for all you've given to this virtual community. There isn't one day that I don't find something interesting, edifying, amusing, even occasionally breathtaking. on this page, all free gifts from you. Also, at this time of giving thanks, I want to say how grateful I am for all the people who work on the holidays: nurses and doctors, police, the people who give us public transportation, wait staff, cooks, and busboys/girls, and so many more. Many work in retail on Thanksgiving, and I wish you didn't have to, but I hope that the day can be structured so that you can enjoy Thanksgiving with your family after your shift is over.

Something comes to mind to me, now, about working on holidays. As a nurse, I often did that, and I didn't really mind it. Bad enough for people to be in the hospital, but to be there on a holiday is really bad. I used to be glad I could offer some help and relief, and then go home to enjoy the rest of the day with my family.

One Christmas, at the hospital where I worked, as many patients as possible had been sent home. So the census was light on our floor; only the sickest remained. My parents worked in a jewelry store at the time, and they gave me a bunch of pins, costume jewelry, but really very pretty, displayed against black velvet, to distribute among the patients. I did so, and many of the women patients pinned them right on their hospital gowns. I felt like Santa Nurse. So it's not always awful to spend time away from your family on a holiday, not if you get to bring some joy and care into another's life. And it's a good reminder that the whole world is our family.

I'm going to Boston for Thanksgiving, and I sure hope the hostess makes a lot of gravy. I also hope she doesn't see how much I use. I put gravy on the gravy.

The (One-sided) Conversation

Gabby, I want to tell you something. I'm going out of town today. I can't bring you with me even though I would really, really like to.....You get to come to South Bend. And for now you'll be here with Bill, okay? It will be fun. It will be *fun*!.......I can't bring you!........Listen, I'm going to foster Goldens after my book tour and you'll have new friends. Won't that be fun? .....It's business. I have to fly. I can't bring you. Okay?

Reaction:

A Note to Youse Guys

My last two years of high school, I spent in St. Louis. We lived next door to a woman named Kathy, and I knew three things about her. One was that she had an at-home job, doing card punching. I did not have the vaguest idea what that was. Card punching? What, you roughed up some cards so that they'd learn the error of their ways?

The second thing I knew about her was that she was a Diet Coke addict, she always had one in her hand or nearby.

The third thing that I knew is that she used to lean her head out the window to call her children home. "Youse guys!" she'd say. "Get in here, now."

If that sounds harsh, it wasn't. It always sounded very friendly to me, a kind of insider language you'd use for people you were very comfortable with.

So it is that I used that term for youse guys, you who read and comment on my Facebook page, and who have created and made sustainable a virtual community where I and others go for all kinds of things: advice, recipes, insight, humor, dog stories, and best of all, friendship.

When my pal Phyllis and I first conceived of publishing select Facebook posts, we had no idea how wonderfully well they'd be received. In our trying to make you happy, you made us so. I'd like to offer sincere and ongoing thanks. I was one of those authors who fought hard against going on Facebook but now I find that I'm...well, happy to be here.

I'll see you on the page.

With love,

Elizabeth Berg is the author of many bestselling novels, as well as two collections of short stories and two works of nonfiction. Open House was an Oprah's Book Club selection, *Durable Goods* and *Joy School* were selected as ALA Best Books of the Year, and *Talk Before Sleep* was short-listed for an Abby Award. *The Pull of the Moon* was adapted into a play and has enjoyed sold out performances in Chicago and Indianapolis. Berg has been honored by both the Boston Public Library and the Chicago Public Library and is a popular speaker at venues across the country. Her work has been translated into 27 languages. Her latest novel, *The Confession Club*, the third set in the town of Mason, will be published in November 2019.

By Elizabeth Berg

Made in United States
Orlando, FL
25 January 2022

14019452R00104